# CHINESE
## *ULTURE*

# PHILOSOPHY

**WU CHUN**

 China Intercontinental Press

图书在版编目（CIP）数据

中国文化 . 哲学思想：英文 / 吾淳著；译谷译 . -- 北京：五洲传播出版社，2014.12

ISBN 978-7-5085-2745-1

Ⅰ . ①中⋯ Ⅱ . ①吾⋯ ②译⋯ Ⅲ . ①文化史－中国－英文②哲学思想－思想史－中国－英文 Ⅳ . ① K203 ② B2-53

中国版本图书馆 CIP 数据核字 (2014) 第 077532 号

--------------------------------------------------------------------------------

**中国文化系列丛书**

主　　　编 ：王岳川
出　版　人 ：荆孝敏
统　　　筹 ：付　平

**中国文化·哲学思想**

著　　　者 ：吾　淳
责 任 编 辑 ：高　磊
译　　　者 ：译　谷
图 片 提 供 ：FOTOE　中新社
装 帧 设 计 ：丰饶文化传播有限责任公司
出 版 发 行 ：五洲传播出版社
地　　　址 ：北京市海淀区北三环中路 31 号生产力大楼 B 座 7 层
邮　　　编 ：100088
电　　　话 ：010-82005927，82007837
网　　　址 ：www.cicc.org.cn
承　印　者 ：北京光之彩印刷有限公司
版　　　次 ：2015 年 5 月第 1 版第 1 次印刷
开　　　本 ：889×1194mm 1/16
印　　　张 ：14
字　　　数 ：200 千字
定　　　价 ：128.00 元

# Contents

# Preface

Chinese philosophy is an extensive and profound subject that has had a deep and lasting impact on China's history and culture. In particular, the advocacy of benevolence, which is a central part of Confucianism and which reflects a broad-minded, virtue-based attitude toward the world, has become a central and highly valued part of the spirit of the nation. At the same time, Taoist wisdom, which is "as infinite as heaven and earth and as inexhaustible as rivers", provides a deep and undying source of motivation for the survival and development of the Chinese nation. Throughout her history, China has returned again and again to those ancient sages and generations of Chinese have reread their classic texts, listened to their teachings, and asked themselves the deep questions that this study has inspired. In fact, Chinese philosophy, based on Confucianism and Taoism, is among the most important and most precious cultural legacies that humankind possesses. The virtue and wisdom it contains can be compared favorably to any other school of philosophy from anywhere else around the world.

As part of the Chinese Culture Series, this book is an introduction to Chinese philosophy structured by subject rather than history. Although this approach makes it impossible to present a complete narrative, this is not a problem. It must be realised that, when looking at over 3,000 years of thinking, many marginal details can be left out without compromising a general, overall understanding of the subject. This is true not only for the history of philosophy, but also for the history of literature, science and art. Hopefully, after having read this book, readers will be left with an exciting impression of the subject, and will be inspired to do further research and reading to get a deeper understanding.

This book is divided into five subjects, which look at five key questions – What is the Nature of the World? What are the Relationships between Things? What are the Social Norms? What is the Proper Orientation of Life? and What is the Structure of Knowledge? In my view, these are the five most basic questions (or subjects) in Chinese philosophy (though they can be broken down into a series of more specific questions). It is worth noting that, of the five subjects mentioned above, the first and the second actually have a profound religious and intellectual background, while the third and the fourth involve social and moral issues. These are the four questions around which many significant thoughts in Chinese philosophy revolve. They are also the four subjects that form the framework of my recent book *The Origin of Chinese Philosophy: the Development and Formation of Ideas, Concepts and Thoughts before the Era of Eastern Zhou Philosophers*. Although these four subjects are key, the fifth 'What is the Structure of Knowledge?' is also very important. It is interesting to note that Taoism places great importance on the first, second and fifth subjects. This is a consequence of its profound intellectual background, as well as its focus on more essential and abstract issues, such as the laws governing the world and the origin of the universe. Although these philosophical issues are difficult to grasp and describe, Taoism presents a unique outlook on knowledge and language. In comparison, Confucianism is more interested in the third, fourth and fifth subjects. This focus is reflected in its theory of self-cultivation, statecraft, and its idea of the combination of "inner sage" and "outer ruler." According to Confucianism, a person's life should begin with "investigating things to achieve knowledge" (*gewu zhizhi*). The aim of this should be to attain an ideal character (becoming the "inner sage") through the moral cultivation of one's self. The eventual goal should be to apply oneself to social practice and to achieve the goal of "regulating the family, ruling the state, and maintaining peace for all under Heaven" (becoming the "outer ruler"). An understanding of these ideas, their structures and their relationships with the other major schools of thought may help with the reading of this book and, in turn, help with the development of a deeper understanding of the essentials of Chinese philosophy.

In order to present a relatively complete overview of Chinese philosophy and its issues, this book uses a combination of ideas, concepts and categories to cover a range of thoughts, theories and doctrines. This multi-faceted approach is taken to make the book as comprehensive as possible and to aid understanding of the concepts it covers. The approach taken is important as if, for example, the book only focused on concepts or categories, it would not provide a clear view of some important theories, and might miss out some of the brilliant discussions that have taken place around a certain issue. On the other hand, a narrative only based on theories and doctrines would miss out many crucial concepts and the important ideas they contain.

Given the limitations of the book's length it was decided that the only viable approach would be to highlight key points, including the thoughts of Confucianism and Taoism, especially those of their founders Confucius and Lao Tzu. It was also decided to focus on the pre-Qin period, during which many of the thoughts and theories of Chinese philosophy were developed (e.g. the Confucian theory of human nature and ideas on character, and Taoist dialectics). The book does give attention to later developments, where appropriate, however, omissions are inevitable, and it is hoped that readers will be inspired to find out more.

There are some other features about the way in which this book has been written that are worth mentioning here. First, I have tried to present Chinese philosophy as it really is. This is important as recently, under the influence of Western philosophy and trends of thought, the way in which issues covered by Chinese philosophy are described, including the terminology that is employed, has become increasingly Westernized, so much so that its identity has been blurred. This book therefore tries to get to the essence of what Chinese philosophy was originally like. It looks at the impact that science has had on its development and looks at the concepts of yin and yang, the Five Elements and Dao and Li. It investigates the close relationship between philosophy and teaching, and how it has been put into practice on a social level. It highlights the special role and significance of musical aesthetics in philosophical thinking, and the relationship of philosophy to the development of belief and knowledge. Furthermore, because of the "international" nature of this book, it also includes some cross-cultural comparisons, which should encourage readers to investigate further for themselves. These comparisons look at areas of disagreement, such as the different attitudes toward Divinity and divination that exist. They also look at areas of commonality, such as the similarity between Chinese family and clan rules and the Jewish Torah regarding ethical issues. Overall, they show that Chinese thinking and philosophy share common ground with other ways of thinking.

I am indebted to Professor Cui Yiming, the co-editor of the textbook – *Chinese Philosophical Ideas* (East China Normal University Press, 1998) – upon which this book is based, for his contribution. In fact, some passages in this book have been directly quoted from the textbook. I would also like to thank Jiang Kaitian, the PhD candidate under my tutelage, who has helped me to collate materials and who has given me some good advice. My thanks also go to China Intercontinental Press (CIP) for giving me this opportunity to introduce Chinese philosophy to the rest of the world and also for supplying the pictures in this book and translating it into English.

# WHAT IS THE NATURE OF THE WORLD?

What is the nature of the world? This question, which concerns phenomena (observable facts or events) and essence (the set of attributes that makes something what it is), is asked in every kind of philosophy. For ancient Western philosophers essence was more important than phenomena (due to factors such as Plato's skepticism about the reliability of phenomena). However, this was not the case for ancient Chinese philosophers, for whom phenomena played as important a role as essence. This chapter starts by considering the issue of *shen* (which can be translated as God, divinity, spirit, or "spiritual power"), which, as we shall see, involves both polytheism and atheism. Then it looks at the concept of yin and yang, and the idea of the Five Elements (*wuxing*). It investigates how the early Chinese people perceived nature, how the two concepts came into being and developed, and how they became central concepts in Chinese philosophy. The third part of this chapter deals with how the ancient Chinese perceived difference and variability, which also gives an insight into how ancient Chinese philosophy addressed the issue of phenomena. Finally, it looks at how Chinese philosophy has considered the issue of essence (which involves the concepts of origin and noumenon and *qi*, *dao*, and *li*, as well as various laws and rules). It highlights an overall movement toward the general and the abstract in the thinking process of the ancient Chinese philosophers.

# The Birth of Beliefs

Like many other ancient nations or civilizations, China developed the idea of *shen* as its first concept and belief. Such belief or worship can be traced back to remote antiquity before the period of "Three Dynasties" (Xia, Shang and Zhou), namely 2070 BC. It was a part of Chinese thinking throughout the country's ancient history. However, by the time of the Spring and Autumn Period (770-476 BC) Chinese intellectuals had begun to show a tendency to deny or downplay the existence of God. The emergence of such rationalism, which was followed by the development of both Taoism and Confucianism, had an immeasurably large impact on China's intellectual community.

## Shen, the Religious Source of Chinese Philosophical Ideas

As far as the written language is concerned, the Chinese character for *shen* ( 神 ) has been frequently found inscribed on oracle bones. However, the idea of *shen* must have come into existence even earlier. This is borne out by an account about the "isolation of Earth from Heaven" which was given by Guan Shefu, a senior official of the state of Chu, to King Zhao of Chu, and which is recorded in *The Discourses of the States* (*Guo Yu*):

Oracle bone recording the worship of "ghost" and "God," unearthed in Yin Ruins, Anyang, Henan Province.

**In ancient times, people and gods were not mingled. Upon those among the people who were**

faithful and solemn, prudent and upright, whose wisdom was exemplary for people of higher and lower status alike, whose sagacity was known far and wide, and whose sight and hearing were extraordinary, the spirits of gods would descend. The male among them were called *xi*, and the female, *wu*. ... Thus there were officials in charge of matters related to heaven, earth, gods, people, and all kinds of things, called the Five Officials, each of whom maintained order in his jurisdiction without any confusion. Owing to this, the people were loyal and faithful, and the gods were virtuous. The people and the gods went about their separate business, respecting each other with no profanity. So the gods blessed the people with a good life, and the people offered sacrifices to the gods, protected as they were from misfortune and shortage. However, when Shao Hao's rule declined, Jiuli began to disrupt the moral order, so that people were mingled with gods, making it impossible to tell them apart. Female magicians were allowed to offer sacrifices to gods, and each family had its own magicians, but no sense of faith and loyalty. People neglected their sacrifices and did not know their blessings. They indulged in excesses and placed themselves on a par with gods. They profaned the sacred oath between man and gods, depriving the latter of their awe-inspiring solemnity. The gods, on their part, also connived with the people's wrongdoings rather than stopping them. As a result, no auspicious crops appeared anymore to be offered to the gods. Moreover, misfortunes befell the people one after another, and there

Rubbings of oracle bone script. These roughly mean: "Should the female slaves be used as sacrifice and offered to the God of the River?"

seemed to be no end to them. When Zhuan Xu came to power, he ordered Zhong, the Official of South, to be in charge of heaven and affairs related to the gods, and ordered Li, the Official of Fire, to be in charge of earth and affairs related to the people, so that the original order was restored to prevent man and gods from mutual encroachment and profanity. This was called "the severing of communication between heaven and earth."

This passage conveys the following general meanings:

1. Male and female priests existed to facilitate communication between divine beings and man (from "In ancient times, people and gods were not mingled" to "The male among them were called *xi*, and the female, *wu*").

2. Official positions were created to put people in charge of this communication (from "Thus there were officials in charge of matters related to heaven, earth, gods, people, and all kinds of things" to "protected as they were from misfortune and shortage").

3. This communication fell into disorder starting from the decline of Shao Hao (from "However, when Shao Hao's rule declined" to "misfortunes befell the people one after another, and there seemed to be no end to them").

4. Order was restored in the reign of Zhuan Xu (from "When Zhuan Xu came to power" to "the severing of communication between heaven and earth").

After the period described in this account, the idea of shen was retained despite the appearance of the concepts of and words for "the supreme being" (*di*) and "heaven" (*tian*). In fact, there are records about such concepts in writings dating from the Shang and Zhou Dynasties: "He then offered a special sacrifice to the Supreme Ruler, sacrificed purely to the six honored ones, looked with devotion to the hills and rivers, and worshipped with distinctive rites the hosts of spirits," (*Canon of Yao, Book of Documents*) and "From these mountains was sent down a Spirit/Who gave birth to [the princes of] Fu and Shen," (*Lofty Mountains, Major Court Hymns, Classic of Poetry*).

Having developed during the Shang and Zhou Dynasties, the idea of divinity became firmly established among the Chinese in subsequent eras. It was reflected in the offerings and sacrifices that the ancient Chinese made to Heaven and Earth, to all deities, and to ancestors – customs through which the concept was formalized and ritualized. Later in China's history the idea was reflected in the polytheistic beliefs of Taoism and Buddhism, which shows the continuity of China's tradition of beliefs[1].

## Atheism

On the other hand, we should be aware that, since the Spring and Autumn Period, Chinese philosophy gradually developed atheistic ideas. Instead of absolutely repudiating the existence of God, this kind of atheism marginalized or weakened the role of God and denied that God had any dominant position or significance. Meanwhile, it explained the universe in terms of nature or laws, or enhanced the role of man and the responsibility he had to bear for himself. This, according to Karl Theodor Jaspers, was a reflection of rationalism[2]. Examples can be found in ancient records, such as the following: Shi Yin said, "When a state is about to rise, the people are listened to; when it is about to fall, divinity is followed." (*Zuo Zhuan, The 32ⁿᵈ Year of the Reign of Duke Zhuang*) Shu

---

1. Here it is safe to extend the discussion of the Chinese people's religious outlook to some degree. Max Weber said that the Chinese people's beliefs are traditional. This remark was undoubtedly made in comparison with Abraham's monotheistic system. According to Zhang Guangzhi, Chinese society is characterized by continuity, which is obviously reflected, among other things, in their attitude toward God. It has to be noted, however, that there is actually no essential difference between the Chinese beliefs and those of ancient Greece and early Rome. However, whereas the religious traditions of Greece and Rome were terminated by the introduction of Christianity (which was based on the revolution of Judaism), those of China have continued to exist. This religious tradition has, naturally, been reflected in the thinking and outlook of the Chinese people. For more discussion of this continuity, you may read my book: *The Religous Tradition of Chinese Society: Opposition and Coexistence between Magic and Ethics*, Shanghai SDX Joint Publishing Company, 2009.

2. Jaspers said that, "with the advent of the "axial age," the age of mythology, along with its serenity and clarity, was gone forever; reason and rationally expounded experience waged a war against mythology". (Karl Jaspers: *The Origin and Goal of History*, Huaxia Press, 1989, p. 9).

*Ximen Bao Demystifying the Superstition that Offered Girls to God of River as Wife* (Comic) . Ximen Bao (475-221 BC) was born in the Wei Kingdom in the Warring States Period. He was an atheist. He was once a magistrate at Yexian County (today in the west of Linzhang County, Hebei Province and north of Anyang, Henan Province), which had been suffering floods. The local witch colluded with the officials and the citizens' wealth. The citizens could not tolerate the burden. Knowing this, Ximen Bao disclosed the scam and educated the citizens. He also issued laws to prohibit witchcraft.

Xing regarded both the fall of a meteorite and the "backward flight of six water fowls" as natural phenomena "related to yin and yang" rather than bad omens. (*The 16ᵗʰ Year of the Reign of Duke Xi*) A comet appeared when Yan Zi was in the state of Qi. When asked by the Marquis of Qi, who saw it as a bad omen, to pray to the gods, Yan Zi said, "If you do not doubt the Way of Heaven and follow its mandate in good faith, why should it be necessary to pray?" (*The 26ᵗʰ Year of the Reign of Duke of Zhao*) Sun Tzu was even more atheistic. He said, "Foreknowledge cannot be obtained from ghosts or spirits, nor from gods, nor by analogy with past events, nor from astrological calculations. It can only come from men who know the enemy's situation." (*The Use of Spies, The Art of War*) This approach is, of course, necessary for military operations, and presents a vivid reflection of a scientific view of military affairs.

Since the late Spring and Autumn Period, this fine tradition of rationalism was carried on by Taoist, Confucian and Legalist scholars. For instance, Confucius' rational opinions on "gods and spirits" are recorded in *The Analects*:

**To keep one's distance from the gods and spirits while showing them reverence can be called wisdom. (*Yong Ye*)**

**The subjects on which the Master did not talk, were: extraordinary things, feats of strength, disorder, and spiritual beings. (*Shu Er*)**

**You don't know yet how to serve men; how can you serve spirits? (*Xian Jin*)**

Here it is obvious that Confucius distanced himself from – or even kept silent about – the issue of gods and spirits. Confucius believed that what was important was not what gods and spirits meant to man, but the meaning of man's own behavior. So did Lao Tzu, as is apparent from these remarks in the *Tao Te Ching*:

**I do not know whose son it is. It might appear to have been before God. (Chapter 4)**

**Let the kingdom be governed according to the Dao, and the manes of the departed will not manifest their spiritual energy. It is not that those manes have not that spiritual energy, but it will not be employed to hurt men. (Chapter 60)**

Though he did not deny the existence of God, it is obvious that Lao Tzu placed God's role below, or behind, that of Dao. In fact, he was not really willing to talk about it. It is also true that such an atheistic attitude is fully reflected in the concept and idea of "nature." This was the nature of the intellectual tradition basically followed by Confucianism and Taoism throughout the pre-Qin period. In comparison, the Legalists were even stronger atheists. For instance, Guan Zi said, "If the land is not properly cultivated and the ruler cannot maintain unity among his people, it would be impossible to prevent the country from falling into danger. If the ruler relies on divination and is fond of listening to magicians, spirits would cause him great trouble." (*Guan Zi, The Development of Power*) Han Fei said, "To go by the divinatory calendar, worship spirits, believe in fortune-telling, and indulge in sacrifices is likely to cause a state to collapse." (*Guan Zi, Indications of Pending Collapse*) Even better known is the story of Ximen Bao's administration of Ye. The concept of divinity was therefore absent from the philosophy of Legalism. It was also absent from the School of Logicians, late Mohism, and the School of Medicine.

After the Qin and Han Dynasties, the ideas of the pre-Qin philosophers fell out of favor, and Taoism was transformed into the Taoist religion, with its atheism replaced by a belief in the existence of God, or even gods. However, the Confucian scholars, whose thoughts had become unified, still basically adhered to the teachings of their predecessors. In particular, in a similar way to Judaists, they remained highly vigilant against and resistant to "illegitimate sacrifices." It is interesting that this approach had a social impact, which is apparent from the precepts and rules of some clans that lived during the Song Dynasty (960-1279) and later times. For instance, *Xinqigong Family Precepts* of the Gao clan in Pangu prohibited witchcraft, the *Family Precepts* of the Long clan in Shouzhou forbade "evil and illicit sacrifices" and the *Clan Prohibitions* of the Li clan of Hejiang forbade its members to "join any secret society or religious organization, or to become a monk." There is no doubt that all these rules reflect the Confucian tradition's deep dissemination into Chinese society. However, due to the concurrent changes that were taking place in China's wider society and culture, this fine tradition of rationalism was almost lost. This was fundamentally due to the strong tradition of polytheistic beliefs in wider Chinese society – beliefs that would not be constrained by the minority opinions of philosophers.

# The Formation of Concepts about Nature

Meanwhile, various concepts about nature were also developed through intellectual endeavour and the observation of the natural world. In China, "yin and yang" and the "Five Elements" are among the oldest and most typical of such concepts. The concept of yin and yang mainly derived from knowledge about "phenomena" (*xiang*), whereas the concept of the Five Elements mainly evolved from knowledge about "categories" (*lei*). However, both concepts contain the vestiges of belief in magic, which has had a profound impact on Chinese philosophy. This is one manifestation of the continuity of Chinese culture.

## Yin and Yang and the Five Elements: the Intellectual Source of Chinese Philosophical Ideas

The predecessor or prototype of the concept of yin and yang is the idea of opposition, which is a key element in the prehistoric development of thought. It probably started from mankind's primeval interest in symmetry and originated from the observations of animals and plants made by primitive people while they were hunting and gathering (as well as the impressions they had of themselves). Besides, the structure of phratric (kinship group) opposition in early society also played a role in the formation of this idea[3].

In China, the formation of the early idea of opposition has already been archaeologically

---

3. This issue has been addressed by many scholars, such as Ernst Grosse and Franz Boas (from the perspective of art history) and Emile Durkheim and Claude Lévi-Strauss (from the perspectives of sociology and anthropology).

Pan Gu, who created the heaven and the earth in Chinese legend. He was a giant who came out when the universe was ruptured and the heaven and the earth formed.

proven. For instance, an early awareness of "more" and "less" is shown in the recording of numbers on ancient bones or wood. The ancient Chinese people must also have had an awareness of good and poor harvests and an awareness of fertility and barrenness through their practice of crop rotation and leaving some fields fallow. They would have had an awareness of "fast" and "slow," or efficiency, through the use of farm tools. They would also have had a grasp of the concepts of "large" and "small," "more" and "less," "deep" and "shallow," and "permanent" and "temporary" thanks to their use of storage. In addition, the contrasts they would have experienced between their stone axes and stone wedges would have given rise to the ideas of "sharp" and "blunt," and "thick" and "thin." The making of pottery would have involved knowledge about fast and slow wheels, upper and lower kiln holes, more and fewer firing cavities, and high and low temperatures. The spinning of yarn would have involved knowledge about large or small, light or heavy, and fast or slow wheels as well as coarse and fine textiles. While construction work would definitely have involved the concepts of dry or damp environments, high or low houses, deep or shallow foundations, and thick or thin and long or short components.

Early Chinese concepts of opposition are also widely reflected in pictures and patterns. For instance, there are symmetrical images of fish and human faces combined with fish painted on the pottery of the Yangshao Culture, while S-shaped patterns ( ∽ ) have been found on the painted pottery of the Qujialing Culture. These patterns could be the original form of the Taichi diagram[4]. The same is true of ancient bronzes, many of which were decorated with symmetrical animal motifs. These, in turn, probably reflect the social structure or system of the time, for the

---

4. See Zhang Pengchuan: *An Illustrated Overview of Chinese Painted Pottery*, Cultural Relics Press, 1990, pp. 184-188.

royal lineage of the Yin Dynasty was divided into two groups – Zhao and Mu[5]. Following pictures, symbols played an important role in the establishment of the idea of opposition and the concept of yin and yang. A discussion of this issue requires us to mention the symbols and in the *Book of Change*. The *Book of Change* was intended to be a book for divination, and the symbols originally represented two possibilities or results – auspiciousness and inauspiciousness. Yet they also alluded to the idea of opposition, as apparent from statements like "the little gone and the great come" and "there is no state of peace that is not liable to be disturbed" (*Hexagram Tai*), and "the great gone and the little come" and "distresses comes before joy" (*Hexagram Pi*). In particular, the symbols have quite obvious links to yin and yang. Hegel said, "Phenomenal manifestations of objects always precede concepts in the human consciousness."[6] Both pictures and symbols are phenomenal manifestations, and they pave the way for concepts. Symbols are better than pictures as the precursors for concepts because they are more abstract and yet more concrete. They also provide more general and more accurate references. In addition they can be used in combination with concepts. This is exactly

Pottery pot with vortex pattern, unearthed in Xichuan, Henan Province. It belonged to the Qujialing Culture of the Neolithic Age that existed 4,800-6,800 years ago. It has a vortex shape. It is now in the collection of the Henan Museum.

---

5. See Zhang Guangzhi: *Fine Arts, Mythology and Sacrifice*, Liaoning Education Press, 1988, pp. 63-64.

6. Hegel: *Die Logik*, Commercial Press, 1981, p. 37.

Illustration in *Three Character Classic for Children Learning with Illustrations*: The Five Elements, drawn by Jinzhang Bookstore in the early Republic of China.

the reason why and would become important symbols for opposition in the Chinese philosophy of later eras.

During this period, there also gradually developed antithetic words that described the concept of yin and yang in a broad sense. Such words can be found in both the *Book of Documents* and the *Book of Change*. Eventually, there appeared the expression "yin and yang" in the phrase "observe its yin and yang" in the poem *Gong Liu* (*Major Court Hymns, Classic of Poetry*). From these beginnings, the philosophical concept of yin and yang became established, as is apparent from the famous discourse by Bo Yangfu, the royal historian of Zhou. He explained the cause of earthquakes in terms of an imbalance between the yin *qi* and the yang *qi*, as recorded in *The Discourse of Zhou* (part 1) in *The Discourses of the States*:

**The *Qi* of heaven and earth normally maintains its own order; if not, it is because the people have caused confusion in it. If yang is pinned down and prevented from exiting, and yin is oppressed and cannot rise, there would be an earthquake. Now the cause of the recent earthquake**

**in the three rivers is that the yang has been dislodged from its proper place and has oppressed the yin. When this happens, the sources of the rivers will be stopped; if so, the kingdom is bound to collapse.**

By the end of the Spring and Autumn Period, plenty of yin-and-yang concepts had appeared in both a broad (i.e. antithetic words) and a more specific sense (i.e. yin-and-yang concepts in a narrower or more abstract sense). Moreover, these concepts were made full use of in pure or relatively pure philosophical thinking. For instance, Sun Tzu said, "Heaven signifies yin and yang, cold and heat, times and seasons" (*Laying Plans, The Art of War*). And Fan Li said, "when yang becomes extreme, it will turn into yin, and vice versa. If we are inferior to the enemy, use the yin strategy (i.e. striking only after the enemy has struck); if we are superior, use the yang strategy (i.e. preemptive strike)" (*The Discourse of Yue II, The Discourses of the States*).

Another type of concept - that is common to many ancient philosophies - takes the form of a cosmic model, or the generalization of the whole world into several things, phenomena or numbers. Though such models differ from nation to nation and from one ethnic group to another, they commonly exist as a basic perception or understanding of the world[7]. One of them is the Chinese concept of the Five Elements.

The concept of the Five Elements can be traced back to the concept of the Four Directions, a clear example of which can be found in the *Classic of Mountains and Seas*. For instance, it is said in the *Classic of Regions beyond the Seas: South* that "Kunlun Mound is in the east and square in shape." Moreover, directions are matched with certain animals, gods and numbers. For example, it is said in the *Classic of the Great Wilderness: East* that the people of Wei lived on millet and could command four kinds of bird as well as tigers, leopards, black bears and brown bears. Archaeological findings also provide some illustrations of the existence of this concept, these include the many cruciform and double-cross (like the Union Jack) patterns on Neolithic painted pottery. Such patterns, which cannot be accidental or meaningless, are thought to reflect a common idea, i.e. the

---

7. Copious accounts of this can be found in *Primitive Mentality* by Lucien Lévy-Bruhl.

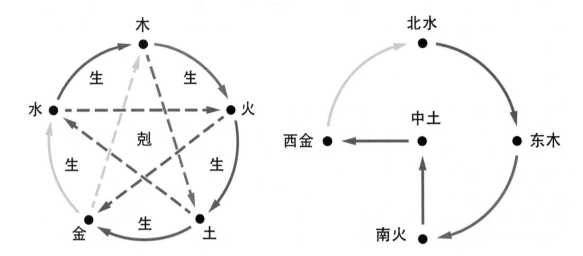

"Chart of the mutual generation and mutual overcoming of the Five Elements," drawn by Cheng Jianjun.

idea of the Four Directions. Established in prehistoric society, this idea was developed during the Three Dynasties (Xia, Shang and Zhou). Additionally, following the founding of a unified dynasty, the awareness of "center" became important. For instance, the concept of "central Shang" had appeared in oracle inscriptions of the time: "Divination conducted on the day of Gengchen, central Shang" (*Yi* 9078). Thus the idea of the Five Directions emerged.

The concept of the Five Elements first appeared in the *Great Plan* in the *Book of Documents*:

**Of the five elements: The first is water; the second is fire; the third, wood; the fourth, metal; and the fifth, earth. (The nature of) water is to soak and descend; of fire, to blaze and ascend; of wood, to be crooked and straight; of metal, to yield and change; while (that of) earth is seen in seed-sowing and in-gathering. That which soaks and descends becomes salt; that which blazes and ascends becomes bitter; that which is crooked and straight becomes sour; that which yields and changes becomes acrid; and from seed-sowing and in-gathering comes sweetness.**

According to current thinking, this passage, which mainly discusses the properties of things or materials, is about grasping the nature of things or the origin of the world.

However, that might not be the original meaning of this concept, which, at the very beginning, was probably related to the ideas of the Five Stars and the Five Materials. With respect to the intellectual background of the term "Five Elements," it is clear that it must be closely related to the craft of astrology, which was highly developed during the Shang and Zhou Dynasties. It is possible that the Five Elements (*wu xing*) originally referred to the Five Stars – *Chen* (Mercury), *Taibai* (Venus), *Yinghuo* (Mars), *Sui* (Jupiter), and *Zhen* (Saturn). The character *xing* in *wu xing* denotes the movement of the stars, or heavenly bodies in general, which was already understood during the Spring and Autumn Period (e.g. "In the movement of the sun and the moon, the ecliptic crosses the equator at the Spring Equinox and the Autumn Equinox, and goes beyond the equator at the Summer Solstice and the Winter Solstice" (*Zuo Zhuan, The 21ˢᵗ Year of the Reign of Duke Zhao*). During the last years of the Western Zhou Dynasty (1046-771BC) there appeared the term "Five Materials," which was already in quite common usage during the Spring and Autumn Period. Examples of its use include: "So one of the early kings mingled earth with metal, wood, water and fire to create everything" (*The Discourses of the States, The Discourse of Zheng*), and "Heaven has created the Five Materials, and the people have to use them all, for each of them is indispensable" (*Zuo Zhuan, The 27ᵗʰ Year of the Reign of Duke Xiang*).

From this it can be imagined that, at first, people might have been more interested in the utilitarian significance of things and materials rather than the origin of the world. Therefore the concept of the Five Elements is actually a combination of the specific concepts of the Five Materials (metal, wood, water, fire and earth) and the Five Stars. This combination potentially indicates that life on earth (as represented by the Five Materials) and events in the sky (as reflected by the Five Stars) were the greatest concerns of people at the time. The former was related to people's interest in the materials of daily life, while the latter was related to the destiny of the state. The combination is clearly described in a remark by Cai Mo, the Grand Historian of the state of Jin (*Zuo Zhuan, The 29ᵗʰ Year of the Reign of Duke Zhao*), "So there were the Five Officials in charge of the Five Elements, who were given clan and family names, made highest-ranking nobles, and worshipped as gods, to whom sacrifices were offered. The official of wood is called Goumang;

the official of fire, Zhurong; the official of metal, Rushou; the official of water, Xuanmin; and the official of earth, Houtu." Here we can see factors relating to materials and their uses, and we can also see astrological elements. Thus the concept of the Five Elements became widely used: "Heaven has six kinds of Qi, which generate the Five Tastes, show the Five Colors, and correspond to the Five Tones" (*The 1st Year of the Reign of Duke Zhao*). "So there are the Three Celestial Bodies in heaven and the Five Elements on earth," (*The 32nd year of the Reign of Duke Zhao*). "There are not more than five musical notes, yet the combinations of these five give rise to more melodies than can ever be heard. There are not more than five primary colors (blue, yellow, red, white, and black), yet in combination they produce more hues than can ever been seen. There are not more than five cardinal tastes (sour, acrid, salt, sweet, bitter), yet combinations of them yield more flavors than can ever be tasted," (*The Art of War, Energy*).

From this point on, the concepts and ideas of yin and yang and the Five Elements would have a profound impact on the whole philosophy of ancient China.

## Vestiges of Magic

However, we should also be aware of the mystic overtones or vestiges of magic that are part of the world view that is based on the concepts of yin and yang and the Five Elements.

---

8. The age-old Chinese tradition of divination can be traced back to the period of the Longshan Culture, when it was mainly conducted using bones. From the Yin and Western Zhou Dynasties till the Spring and Autumn Period, Chinese divination was mainly conducted using either tortoise shells or Achillea stalks. The chapter *Great Plan* in the *Book of Documents* contains the following words: "Of the (means for the) examination of doubts – Officers having been chosen and appointed for divining by the tortoise-shell (*bu*) and the stalks of the Achillea (*shi*), they are to be charged (on occasion) to execute their duties. (In doing this), they will find (the appearances of) rain, of clearing up, of cloudiness, of want of connection, and of crossing; and the inner and outer diagrams. In all (the indications) are seven: five given by the shell, and two by the stalks; and (by means) of these errors (in the mind) may be traced out." Here *bu* means divination by the tortoise shell and *shi* means divination by Achillea stalks. "Rain," "clearing up," "cloudiness," "want of connection" and "crossing" are the five indications given by the former, and "inner and outer diagrams" are the two indications given by the latter.

The Eight Trigrams (*Bagua*). The *Yin* and *Yang* pictures in the middle are commonly called *Yin-Yang* Fish, and the surrounding symbols stand for the Eight Trigrams.

As mentioned before, one of the major sources of the concept of yin and yang is the *Book of Change*, which was used for divination[8]. The basic symbols in the *Book of Change*, which originally represented a long bamboo tube (or a long blade of yarrow) and two short bamboo tubes (or two short blades of yarrow) respectively, stand for two results: auspiciousness and inauspiciousness, or benefit and harm. At first, each attempt at divination was only done once. However, people found this too haphazard, and divination began to be done twice or thrice at a time. The adoption of three-time divination was an important step, as it was not so haphazard as one-time divination, or as likely to have contradictory results as two-time divination. Hence the saying that "divination should not be done more than three times." Nevertheless, divination would, on occasion, be repeated four, five or even six times. As a result of this repetitive divination people began to notice the possible permutations of — and -- . Three-time divination was bound to produce eight results (☰ ☷ ☳ ☵ ☶ ☴ ☲ ☱), or the Eight Trigrams (Bagua) as they were called. Similarly, six-time divination would produce 64 kinds of result, hence the 64 Trigrams. It is thought that obtaining the 64 Trigrams might mainly (or purely) have been the result of an interest in permutations rather than

divination. To sum up, the *Book of Change* was a book for divination. As such it has always been regarded as the most important of all the Chinese traditional classics. As *Commentaries on Book of Change* puts it,

> **The Yi was made on a principle of accordance with heaven and earth, and shows us therefore, without rent or confusion, the course (of things) in heaven and earth. (*Xi Ci I*)**
>
> **It was by the Yi that the sages exalted their virtue, and enlarged their sphere of occupation. (ditto)**

In the period when metaphysics was in vogue during the Wei and Jin Dynasties, the *Book of Change* was one of the "three metaphysical classics" (the other two being *Tao Te Ching* and *Chuang Tzu*). Today it is still regarded as a milestone in the history of Chinese philosophy. It shows that the intellectuals and thinkers of the time, who would have formed the most rational group in society, had still maintained a close relationship with traditional beliefs and had not totally broken with the tradition of divination or magic. This state of affairs was bound to have a profound impact on Chinese philosophical ideas and thinking[9].

The same is true of the concept of the Five Elements. As discussed before, this concept originated from knowledge about directions and divination, which was related, to varying degrees, with religious activities and beliefs. Having developed during the Spring and Autumn Period, the concept gave rise to the School of Yin, Yang and Five Elements during the Warring States Period. This school enjoyed considerable prestige for some time. It was characterized, above all else, by its desire to match up all kinds of natural phenomena, such as directions, seasons, colors, tastes, musical tones and numbers, with deities. Central to these relationships was the concept of the Five Elements. For instance, it is said in the chapter *Proceedings of Government in the Different Months* in the *Book of Rites* that:

---

9. In sharp contrast to this, divination was absolutely rejected or banned in Abraham's religious system. This was also regarded as a kind of "disenchantment" by Max Weber.

**(In the first month of spring) ... Its days are Jia and Yi. Its divine ruler is Tai Hao, and the (attending) spirit is Goumang. Its creatures are the scaly. Its musical note is Jue, and its pitch-tube is the Taicu. Its number is eight; its taste is sour; its smell is rank.**

The same words are found in the chapter *Records on the First Month of Spring* in *The Annals of Lü Buwei*. Afterwards, such theories had a deep influence on intellectual activities, which made them inevitably mystic to some degree. For instance, the East corresponds to the color blue and is related to the liver that opens into the eyes and stores Jing (Essence). The manifestation of liver disease is fright. In terms of its analogies, the liver is related to sour tastes, to grasses and trees (in

The Twenty-eight Constellations on the cover of the tomb of the Wang family from the Southern Tang Dynasty, unearthed in an ancient tomb in Hanjiang, Jiangsu Province in 1964. It was carved in 946, the 4th year of Baoda Period of the Southern Tang Dynasty. Inside the top cover were carved the sun, the moon, the Huagai Star, the Gouchen Star, and the Eight Trigrams. In the middle, the Chinese zodiac was carved. On the outside were carved the Twenty-eight Constellations. Around the tomb were craved an Azure Dragon, a White Tiger, a Vermilion Bird, and a Black Tortoise.

the category of wood), to chicken (in the category of domestic animals), to wheat (in the category of crops), to Jupiter (in the category of stars), to the Jiao scale, to the number eight and to foul smells, (*The Inner Canon of the Yellow Emperor, Basic Questions, Discussion on the Important Ideas in the Golden Chamber*). East also corresponds to wood and the Emperor Taihao. His assistant was Goumang, who traditionally is meant to have ruled spring with a pair of compasses. East is also related to the god Suixing (Jupiter), the Black Dragon, the tone Jue, and the days of Jia and Yi (*Huai Nan Zi, Treatise on Astronomy*). By this time the theory of the Five Elements had become a completely cosmic model containing a miscellany of mystic and fantastic beliefs.

Incidentally, it is worth mentioning that, following the introduction of Buddhism and the birth of Taoism, such mystic thoughts would have a profound impact on ideas and knowledge. For instance, though Chinese medicine began to eschew magic as early as in the pre-Qin period, it began to embrace superstitions about spirits and karmic retribution during the Tang Dynasty due to the introduction of Buddhist incantations. This was actually a reversal back to magic.

# Observation and Thinking about Phenomena

The Chinese way of thinking had grown through observation from its very beginning, which is a process that has also had an impact on philosophical thinking. The vast majority of Chinese philosophers have not thought about any issue in isolation from phenomena, and this can be said to be an important feature of Chinese philosophy.

## The Concept of Difference or Diversity

One of the first consequences of observing phenomena is that one is aware of the amazing variety in the world, which gives rise to the idea of difference or diversity. (In fact, we can already find the ideas of difference or diversity in the Chinese concepts of "yin and yang" and the Five Elements.) As a result of such early observations, there appeared a Chinese word related to this idea, "harmony" (*he*). The earliest Chinese concept of "harmony" was related to musical aesthetics and can be traced back to *Canon of Yao in the Book of Documents*:

**Poetry is the expression of earnest thought; singing is the prolonged utterance of that expression; the notes accompany that utterance, and they are harmonized themselves by the standard-tubes. (In this way) the eight different kinds of musical instruments can be adjusted so that one shall not take from or interfere with another; and spirits and men are brought into harmony.**

The huge stone inscription of the Chinese character 和 (*He*, Harmony) on a cliff at the Hanging Monastery, Hengshan Mountain, Shanxi Province. The Hanging Monastery is the only existing temple that is worshipped by Buddhism, Taoism, and Confucianism in China. The smaller words read "Hengshan Mountain is one of the Five Famous Mountains in China, where Buddhism, Taoism, and Confucianism co-exist. Harmony is the eternal theme of humankind."

Here we see phrases like "they are harmonized themselves by the standard-tubes" and "the eight different kinds of musical instruments can be adjusted." We also see the two important concepts of "harmony" (*he*) and "accord" (*xie*), which were used to describe the kind of harmony that was expected to exist between musical tones and between musical instruments.

The Spring and Autumn Period saw a deepening of the understanding of the concept of diversity in China. This understanding was most typically represented by the discourses of Shi Bo and Yan Ying. The words of the former are recorded in The *Discourse of Zheng* in The *Discourses of the States*:

Harmony leads to growth and development, while sameness would put an end to it. To combine one thing with another on an equal footing is called harmony. As such it can stimulate the growth of things. If you try to make up for the deficiency of something with the same thing, it would come to an end and be abandoned. So ancient rulers combined earth with metal, wood, water and fire to create all things in the world ... Such is the apex of harmony. So ancient kings married women from different clans, sought wealth from across the land, and selected officials and advisors to deal with all kinds of affairs, in order to achieve an harmonious governance. A single sound cannot be pleasant to hear, a single color cannot make a beautiful design, a single taste cannot make fine food, and a single thing in isolation from others cannot be evaluated. If the ruler eschews harmony and seeks only sameness, heaven would deprive him of the capacity for sound judgment. If so, how could he avoid pitfalls?

Yan Ying's words are found in *The 20ᵗʰ Year of the Reign of Duke Zhao in Zuo Zhuan*:

Harmony can be compared to thick soup, in which fish and meat are cooked together with water, sauce, salt and plums, heated with firewood underneath. The chef would mix them well, compensating for what is lacking and reducing what is excessive. Such soup, when served to the gentleman, could bring serenity to his mind. The same is true of the relationship between the ruler and his ministers. What the ruler approves of may have something objectionable in it, and his ministers may offer to rectify that so as to make the whole thing approvable; what the ruler disapproves of may have something approvable in it, and his ministers may point this out so that he might change his mind. … But things are different nowadays. What the ruler approves of, his ministers also approve of; what the ruler disapproves of, his ministers also disapprove of. This is like cooking water in water – what could eat it? – or like playing the same tune on the lute and the zither – what could enjoy that kind of music?

Both Shi Bo and Yan Ying were expressing the idea of embracing diversity and opposing uniformity. Specifically speaking, they expressed two main ideas:

1) They gave reasons for opposing uniformity: "Sameness would put an end to [development and growth]" and "If you try to make up for the deficiency of something with the same thing, it would come to end and be abandoned." Here "uniformity" also has two meanings: invariability ("A single sound cannot be pleasant to hear, a single color cannot make a beautiful design, a single taste cannot make fine food, and a single thing in isolation from others cannot be evaluated.") and sameness ("This is like cooking water in water – what could eat it? – or like playing the same tune on the lute and the zither – what could enjoy that kind of music?").

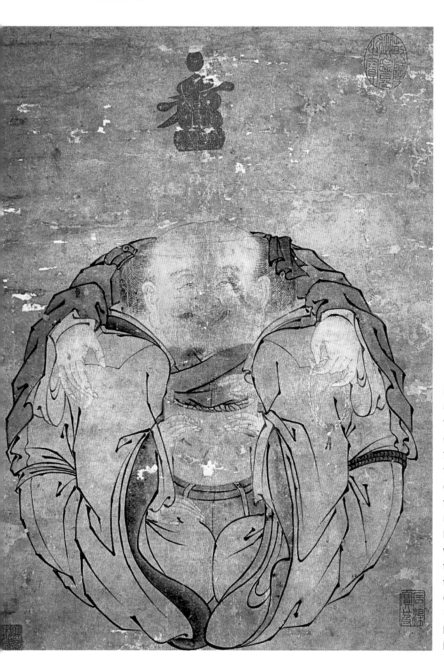

*Harmony*. In this picture, there seems to be a Maitreya who has a round posture and sits with his legs crossed. Upon close inspection, one may find that there are actually three figures. On the left is an old Taoist and on the right is a young Confucian. Both take one end of the script, touch each other with the leg, and smile at each other. In the middle, a man with a bare head puts his hands on their shoulders. He twists beads with his fingers. He is a Buddhist. With these funny characters, the picture indicates the union among Buddhism, Taoism, and Confucianism. It was said to be painted in 1465 by Zhu Jianshen, Emperor Xianzong of Ming Dynasty. It is part of the collection of the Palace Museum.

2) They explained that they embraced diversity because it can "stimulate the growth of things." That is to say, they believed that different things can generate, support or complement each other and that only in this way would it be possible to compensate for weaknesses and "bring all kinds of things into existence."

Such discourses contain the profound observation that no category of things can be perfect and represent everything. It is noteworthy that both Shi Bo and Yan Ying used the concept of "harmony" in their discussion of difference. It is also noteworthy that it has a very clear meaning in this context – unity of diversity[10].

Such an understanding of the objective world would translate into a method of subjective thinking characterized by careful attention to difference. Here Sun Tzu's thoughts provide a case in point. For instance, he noted that one must take into full consideration different topographic and geographic conditions before choosing the proper military approach:

**The natural formation of the country is the soldier's best ally; but a power of estimating the adversary, of controlling the forces of victory, and of shrewdly calculating difficulties, dangers and distances, constitutes the test of a great general. (*Terrain, The Art of War*)**

Sun Tzu's understanding of geographic and topographic differences is mainly reflected in two chapters of The *Art of War – Terrain and The Nine Situations*. In the first of these chapters, terrain is divided into six categories:

*We may distinguish six kinds of terrain, to wit:*

*(1) Accessible ground; (2) entangling ground; (3) temporizing ground; (4) narrow passes; (5) precipitous heights; (6) positions at a great distance from the enemy.*

The second Sun Tzu proposes nine situations:

---

10. Later Chinese philosophers developed a way of thinking known as "synthesis" (canhe). See the next chapter for details.

*The art of war recognizes nine varieties of ground: (1) dispersive ground; (2) facile ground; (3) contentious ground; (4) open ground; (5) ground of intersecting highways; (6) serious ground; (7)difficult ground; (8) hemmed-in ground; (9) desperate ground.*

*If this is not a quote but rather an interjection by the author, it should not be in italics.*

*Replace comma with colon at end of "instance".*

*Therefore, on dispersive ground, I would inspire my men with unity of purpose. On facile ground, I would see that there is close connection between all parts of my army.*

*On contentious ground, I would hurry up my rear.*

*On open ground, I would keep a vigilant eye on my defenses. On ground of intersecting highways, I would consolidate my alliances.*

*On serious ground, I would try to ensure a continuous stream of supplies. On difficult ground, I would keep pushing on along the road.*

*On hemmed-in ground, I would block any way of retreat. On desperate ground, I would proclaim to my soldiers the hopelessness of saving their lives. (The Nine Situations)*

As we can see, Sun Tzu has first made a fine distinction between geographic and topographic conditions, he has then proposed principles of operation suited to each different condition. His advice would make any military operation well-targeted and scientific, thereby improving the possibility of victory[11].

## The Concept of Change or Changeability

Phenomena are not only diverse but are also changeable. As was the case with the concept of diversity, the concept of changeability was gradually acquired by Chinese thinkers through the

---

11. Such a well-targeted method is closely related to the way of thinking that is based on "appropriateness." See relevant contents in the next chapter.

a process of careful observations. Sunrise and sunset, the waxing and waning of the moon, the flourishing and withering of leaves, and the blossom and fall of flowers – all these processes leave a deep impression on people, especially when they are children. The same is true of society, which is always changing. Gradually, the observation of such changeable phenomena led to the formation of the concept of change. For instance, people of the Zhou Dynasty realized that "the mandate of Heaven is not unchangeable." (*King Wen, Major Court Hymns, Book of Poetry.*) For them, the mandate of Heaven would often change and it was never held by any particular ruler for good. Rulers of the Spring and Autumn Period had an even deeper understanding of this, as is apparent from Shi Mo's remark:

*There is no unchanging group of people who offer sacrifices to God of Land and God of Grain, and rulers and their subjects do not have fixed positions. This has been so since ancient times.*

*The descendants of the Three Kings have become commoners. (Zuo Zhuan, The 32nd year of the Reign of Duke Zhao)*

Afterwards, during the Warring States Period, the Legalists developed this idea into an historical outlook that was based on change. For instance, Shang Yang said, "In remote antiquity people were devoted to their loved ones and cared about their private interests; in later antiquity people admired sages and advocated benevolence; in recent times people have come to revere the powerful and defer to officials." (*Opening and Debarring, The Book of Lord Shang*)

During the period of intellectual development that flourished in the late pre-Qin period, philosophers formed opinions on the change of all things in the world. Xun Zi said,

*Stars revolve around each other, the sun and the moon shine upon the earth alternately, the four seasons control the solar terms one by one, yin and yang generate everything in the world, upon which wind and rain are generously bestowed. All things come into being out of the harmony between yin and yang, and develop to their maturity thanks to their nourishment. (Xun Zi, Treastise on Heaven)*

Among these opinions, the understanding of change in the *Book of Change* and the *Commentaries on Book of Change* is particularly insightful and worth cherishing. For instance,

Chinese paper cutting of the Chinese Zodiac Dragon.

Hexagram Qian describes changes in the dragon's position. The line statement (*yaoci*) for the first Nine goes, "The dragon lying hidden (in the deep). It is not the time for active doing." The line statement for the second Nine goes, "The dragon appearing in the field. It will be advantageous to meet with the great man." For the fourth Nine, "The dragon looks as if he were leaping up, but still in the deep. There will be no mistake." For the fifth, "The dragon is on the wing in the sky. It will be advantageous to meet with the great man." For the sixth (topmost), "The dragon exceeding the proper limits, there will be occasion for repentance."

In a similar way, Hexagram Jian describes changes in the position of wild geese. The line statement for the first Six goes, "The wild geese gradually approach the shore." For the second Six, "The geese gradually approach the large rocks." For the third, "The geese gradually advance to the dry plains." For the sixth (topmost), "The geese gradually approach to the large heights." Here we can clearly see how things change. Based on these, the *Commentaries on Book of Change* differentiates various forms of change. For instance it describes changes in society and history in the following way:

> The murder of a ruler by his minister, or of his father by a son, is not the result of the events of one morning or one evening. The causes of it have gradually accumulated. (*Hexagram Kun, Wen Yan*)

> Heaven and earth undergo their changes, and the four seasons complete their functions. Thang changed the appointment (of the line of Hsia to the throne), and Wu (that of the line of Shang), in

accordance with (the will of) Heaven, and in response to (the wishes of) men. Great indeed is what takes place in a time of change. (*Hexagram Ge, Tuan Zhuan*)

The former describes a slow and silent process, while the latter is about revolution. Based on these, the *Commentaries on Book of Change* makes a number of classic statements about change:

The daily renovation which it produces is what is meant by 'the abundance of its virtue.' Production and reproduction is what is called (the process of) change. (*Xi Ci I*)

The Yi (*Book of Change*) is a book which should not be let slip from the mind. Its method (of teaching) is marked by the frequent changing (of its lines). They change and move without staying (in one place), flowing about into any one of the six places of the hexagram. They ascend and descend, ever inconstant. The strong and the weak lines change places, so that an invariable and compendious rule cannot be derived from them; it must vary as their changes indicate. (*Xi Ci II*)

Such classic statements would have a far-reaching impact on later thinking. Meanwhile, *Commentaries on Book of Change* is also aware of the complexity of change and calls it *shen* (spirit, or spiritual power), e.g.:

That which is unfathomable in (the movement of) the inactive and active operations is (the presence of a) spiritual (power). (*Xi Ci I*)

When we speak of Spirit (*shen*) we mean the subtle (presence and operation of God) with all things. (*Shuo Gua*)

That is to say, change is wonderful and unfathomable. *Commentaries* on *Book of Change* also emphasizes "timeliness," i.e. correspondence between human activities and changes in the objective world, e.g.:

Their changes, however varied, are according to the requirements of the time (when they take place). (*Xi Ci II*)

The six lines are mixed together, according to the time (when they enter the figure) and their substance (as whole and divided). (ditto)

In fact, this is a common idea shared by all Chinese.

Since then, many philosophers have given some thought to the different types of change, such as Fan Zhen's idea of "gradual change," Zhang Zai's idea of "change" and "transformation," Zhu Xi's idea of "gradual transformation" and "abrupt change". In particular, Wang Fuzhi's idea that "the form remains the same though the substance changes everyday" (*Thoughts and Questions, External Chapters*) implies that he had considered the relationship between quantitative change and qualitative change.

## Sameness and Difference, Constancy and Change

However, difference and change are not the only considerations when observing and thinking about phenomena.

There is a Chinese concept that is the opposite of difference – sameness (*tong*). This word was already in wide use during the Spring and Autumn Period, as is apparent from the previous quotations from Shi Bo: "Harmony leads to growth and development, while sameness would put an end to it," and "If you try to make up for the deficiency of something with the same thing, it would come to end and be abandoned." During the Warring States Period, "sameness and difference" became a special pair of categories and an important issue of interest for philosophy. For instance, Hui Shi said,

*(When it is said that) things greatly alike are different from things a little alike, this is what is called making little of agreements and differences; (when it is said that) all things are entirely alike or entirely different, this is what is called making much of agreements and differences. (Chuang*

*Tzu, All Under Heaven)*

Xun Zi said,

*The same names should be given to the same things, and different names should given to different things. ... Thus, to avoid confusion, just as things that are the same in substance must have the same names, so things that differ in substance must have different names. (Xun Zi, Rectifying Names)*

In fact, this issue was also of common interest for many scholars and schools of thought, including Gongsun Long and the late Mohists. It was also the subject of many academic works, such as *The Annals of Lü Buwei*. It is also noteworthy that the concept of sameness is closely related

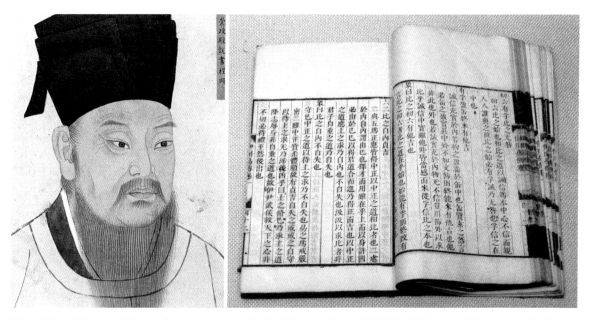

Cheng Yi and *Cheng's Notes on Commentaries on Book of Change*. Cheng Yi (1033-1107) was a philosopher in the School of Mind during the Northern Song Dynasty. *Cheng's Notes on Commentaries on Book of Change*, also known as *Mr. Yichuan's Interpretation of Commentaries on Book of Change*, was a philosophical work in which Cheng Yi annotated the *Book of Change*. It contained views on *Yin* and *Yang*, movement and stillness, reason and desire, and represented Cheng Yi's systematic philosophical thoughts on the universe, nature, society, and life.

to that of lei, which includes categorization, comparison and analogy. All of these involve the issue of sameness, or the issue of sameness and difference. Plenty of discussions on categorization can be found in the thoughts of Gongsun Long, the late Moists and Xun Zi, and in *The Annals of Lü Buwei*. For instance:

**Ming (name): Unrestricted; classifying; private. (*The Book of Mozi, Canon I*)**

**Things of different categories cannot be compared. (*Canon II*)**

*The Book of Mozi* also contains reflections on how the concept of "category" is related to the issue of sameness and difference:

**Tong (same): Identical, as units, as together, of a kind. (*Canon I*)**

**Yi (different): Two, not units, not together, not of a kind. (*Canon I*)**

Constancy (*chang*) is a concept that is the opposite of change. Lao Tzu said, "The report of that fulfilment is the regular, unchanging rule (*chang*)." (*Tao Te Ching*, Chapter 16) Xun Zi said, "Heavenly movements follow constant rules", and "Heaven has a constant rule (to follow), and Earth has constant numbers," (*Xun Zi, Treatise on Heaven*). Thus "constancy and change" form a pair of categories (in the same way as sameness and difference), which were specifically explained by some philosophers. Han Fei said, "That which exists for some time and then disappears, which lives and dies, or which prospers and declines, cannot be said to be constant. Only that which was born when heaven was separated from earth, and which will not decline or die till the disappearance of heaven and earth, can be said to be constant," (*Han Fei Zi, Explaining Lao Tzu*). Meanwhile, the issue of constancy and change is also closely related to the issue of "movement and stillness." For instance, a debater of the Warring States Period proposed that, "The shadow of a flying bird is not in motion," (*Chuang Tzu, All under Heaven*). Seng Zhao, a Buddhist philosopher of the Eastern Jin

Dynasty, wrote *On the Unchangeableness of Things*, in which he said, "The tornado that can topple a hill is always still; racing rivers do not flow; hot air rising in the wilderness does not move; and the sun and the moon, though traveling across the sky, never make a circuit." All such discourses and thoughts deeply touch upon the issue of movement and stillness. Furthermore, this issue is closely related to the origin of the universe. Both Lao Tzu and *Commentaries on Book of Change* believed that stillness is the root of movement. Lao Tzu said, "This returning to their root is what we call the state of stillness," (*Tao Te Ching*, Chapter 16). *Commentaries on Book of Change* says that *Book of Change* was the result of "meditation in stillness that resulted in a thorough understanding of the world," (*Xi Ci I*). However, some philosophers believed the opposite. One of them was Wang Fuzhi, who said,

> **Movement and stillness are caused by the opening and closing [of Taichi]. From closing to opening, from opening to closing – it is movement either way. (*Thoughts and Questions, Inner Chapters*)**

Furthermore, both "sameness" and "constancy" involve the essence or law of things or the world. This subject is discussed below.

# The Quest for Essence and Laws

Alongside the attention they paid to phenomena, ancient Chinese philosophers also reflected upon the general issues that lay behind such phenomena. Such reflections went in two directions: 1) a quest to understand laws or rules, and 2) a quest to understand the ideas of origin and noumenon.

Comparisons show that no philosophical thought has been specifically given to the issue of laws or rules, which has to do with different knowledge backgrounds. While Western ontology largely developed against the background of the study of the issue of attributes, Chinese thoughts about "origin" related to astrology or astronomy. These disciplines provided a background of knowledge and an understanding of natural laws. Moreover, the Western approach was atomistic while the Chinese approach was based on *yuanqi* (vitality or vigor). It is true, however, that both involved the study of the relationship between matter and spirit and the relationship between the specific and the general.

## Dao

The first important concept relating to the ideas of origin and laws is Dao.

The concept of Dao can be found in such early writings as the *Book of Documents* and the *Book of Change*, in which it means "way." Since the late Western Zhou Dynasty, following the development of astrology and astronomy, the word *tiandao*, or the Heavenly Way, became widely used. In *The 9th year of the Reign of Duke Xiang* by Zuo Zhuan, Shi Ruo replies to the Marquis of Jin's question about the Heavenly Way:

*Ebo, Tao Tang Shi's Official of Fire, lived in Shangqiu and offered sacrifices to the Great Fire*

*Asking the Heaven,* drawn by Xiao Yuncong during the Qing Dynasty in 1596. In the middle of the top, there is a *Yin-Yang* symbol that shows how the ancient Chinese understood the origin of the universe. On the left is the sun, represented by the three-legged bird. On the right is the moon, represented by the Jade Hare. In the middle of the bottom, there is a square matrix that stands for the land. Around the matrix are the symbols for the Eight Trigrams that the ancient Chinese used to interpret the laws for changes in the universe and society. The circles that are connected by the short lines are the Twenty-eight Constellations. The 12 animals represent the 12 two-hour periods of the day.

*(Antares) and devised a calendar based on its movement. He was succeeded by Xiangtu, who carried on this practice. As a result, it became the main god worshipped by the Shang Dynasty. Based on their knowledge of the Heavenly Way, the Shang people believed that the collapse of the dynasty was bound to start with some calamity related to fire.*

During the same period the concept of Dao evolved to directly refer to the laws of movement of the heavenly bodies:

*In the movement of the sun and the moon, the ecliptic crosses the equator at the Spring Equinox and the Autumn Equinox, and goes beyond the equator at the Summer Solstice and the Winter Solstice.*

Here the word *fen* was used to refer to the Spring Equinox and the Autumn Equinox, the word *zhi* was used to refer to the Winter Solstice and the Summer Solstice, and the word *dao* was used to refer to the ecliptic and the equator.

Lao Tzu was the first philosopher to regard Dao as the highest philosophical category and to make a systematic study of it. It is noteworthy that his concept of Dao is closely related to the Heavenly Way and to cosmological knowledge.

First of all, let us consider Dao in relationship to his views on the Heavenly Way. Lao Tzu said,

In Heaven there is Dao, and Dao endures long; and to the end of his bodily life, is exempt from all danger of decay. (*Tao Te Ching*, Chapter 16)

How still it was and formless, standing alone, and undergoing no change, reaching everywhere and in no danger (of being exhausted)! (Chapter 25)

Great, it passes on (in constant flow). Passing on, it becomes remote. Having become remote, it returns. (ditto)

The movement of the Dao

By contraries proceeds. (Chapter 40)

The concept of Dao in these quotations was actually directly derived from the idea of the Heavenly Way that existed from the Western Zhou Dynasty to the Spring and Autumn Period. To be more exact, the intellectual source or background of this idea was astrology or astronomy, which developed rapidly to an advanced level during the Spring and Autumn Period. From this perspective, "In Heaven there is Dao, and Dao endures long" means that all heavenly bodies move according to their laws, one of the basic features of which is periodical and circulatory movement. "Great, it passes on (in constant flow). Passing on, it becomes remote. Having become remote, it returns" and "The movement of the Dao/By contraries proceeds" also describe the periodic movement of the heavenly bodies. At that time, the Chinese knew about the periodic movement of the Twelve Stars and the Twenty-eight Constellations. They also knew about the tropical year of the sun and the cycles of the five planets. It is therefore possible to see a clear logical process that led from the intellectual background of the Heavenly Way to Lao Tzu's concept of Dao.

Next, let us consider Dao in the cosmological sense. Understanding of this aspect of the concept generally unfolded in two ways. The first way related to conjecture about the structure or appearance of the universe. Lao Tzu said,

We look at it, and we do not see it, and we name it 'the Equable.' We listen to it, and we do not hear it, and we name it 'the Inaudible.' We try to grasp it, and do not get hold of it, and we name it 'the Subtle.' With these three qualities, it cannot be made the subject of description; and hence we blend them together and obtain The One. Its upper part is not bright, and its lower part is not obscure. Ceaseless in its action, it yet cannot be named, and then it again returns and becomes nothing. This is called the Form of the Formless, and the Semblance of the Invisible; this is called the Fleeting and Indeterminable. We meet it and do not see its Front; we follow it, and do not see its Back. (Chapter 14)

> Who can of Dao the nature tell?
>
> Our sight it flies, our touch as well.
>
> Eluding sight, eluding touch,
>
> The forms of things all in it crouch;
>
> Eluding touch, eluding sight,
>
> There are their semblances, all right.
>
> Profound it is, dark and obscure;
>
> Things' essences all there endure.
>
> Those essences the truth enfold
>
> Of what, when seen, shall then be told. (Chapter 21)

It should be noted that, due to the limited scientific knowledge of the time, the quest to understand the state or appearance of the universe could only lead to a hazy perception or impression of reality – "eluding touch, eluding sight" and "profound it is, dark and obscure." Furthermore, such an impression was bound to involve the issue of language. The most typical and most often quoted words are:

> The Dao that can be trodden is not the enduring and unchanging Dao. The name that can be named is not the enduring and unchanging name. (Chapter 1)

> **I do not know its name, and I give it the designation of the Dao (the Way or Course). Making an effort (further) to give it a name I call it The Great. (Chapter 25)**

This is because the structure or appearance of the universe was, for the ancient Chinese, beyond the scope of their experience. It was therefore "transcendental," and, as such, was very difficult to speak of.

The other way in which the understanding of Dao (in the cosmological sense) unfolded related to conjecture about the origin and evolution of the universe. Lao Tzu said,

> **(Conceived of as) having no name, it is the Originator of heaven and earth; (conceived of as) having a name, it is the Mother of all things. (Chapter 1)**
>
> **There was something undefined and complete, coming into existence before Heaven and Earth. (Chapter 25)**
>
> **All things under heaven sprang from It as existing (and named); that existence sprang from It as non-existent (and not named). (Chapter 40)**
>
> **The Dao produced One; One produced Two; Two produced Three; Three produced All things. (Chapter 42)**

Here the idea is that the universe has developed from nothingness to existence, from less to more, and from "one" to "myriad."

More importantly, however, it is clear that Lao Tzu's concept of Dao transcended the concept of the Heavenly Way and cosmology. It also went beyond the limits of the astronomical knowledge of his time. In his thinking, Lao Tzu had found what lay beyond existing views on the Heavenly Way and cosmology. His concept of Dao therefore had a more "universal" significance in terms of law and origin.

Afterwards, Chuang Tzu carried on Lao Tzu's line of thinking, saying, "The Dao ... has Its root and ground (of existence) in Itself. Before there were heaven and earth, from of old, there It was, securely existing. From It came the mysterious existences of spirits, from It the mysterious existence of God. It produced heaven; It produced earth," (*The Great and Most Honored Master, Chuang Tzu*). However, he noted that there is no distinction between Dao and "matter," for Dao exists in matter or, in his words, "That which makes things what they are has not the limit which belongs to things," (*Knowledge Rambling in the North*). This is where he differed from Lao Tzu. Still later, *Commentaries on Book of Change* also treated Dao as the highest category:

> **Therefore in (the system of) the Yi there is the Grand Terminus, which produced the two elementary Forms. Those two Forms produced the Four emblematic Symbols, which again produced the eight Trigrams. The eight trigrams served to determine the good and evil (issues of events), and from this determination was produced the (successful prosecution of the) great business (of life). (*Xi Ci I*)**

Here "the Great Terminus" (Taiji) means the same as Dao, which is the origin of everything in the universe. Another remark goes,

> **Hence that which is antecedent to the material form exists, we say, as an ideal method (Dao), and that which is subsequent to the material form exists, we say, as a definite thing (Qi). (*Xi Ci I* )**

That is to say, the universe, which was originally formless, is called Dao, whereas everything in it, which has form, is called Qi. Thus Dao and Qi also formed a pair of categories. Philosophers of later times, such as Zhu Xi and Wang Fuzhi, expressed a number of different opinions on these concepts. Additionally, *The Annals of Lü Buwei* used the word *yuandao* (circular Dao) to describe the circulatory nature of the law governing the heavens:

> The alternation between day and night follows the Circular Way; the moon, which moves across the Twenty-eight Constellations, such as Zhen and Jiao, also follows the Circular Way. (*The Circular Way*)

The Wei and Jin Dynasties marked the last stage in the development of the theory of Dao. During this period, the philosopher Wang Bi gave a new explanation of Dao. With respect to the theory of Dao, previous philosophers had mainly been interested in how the universe came into being (i.e. the origin of the universe). In other words, they had considered the relationship between Dao and matter in terms of sequence. Unlike them, Wang Bi showed an interest in ontological issues. That is to say, he considered the relationship between Dao and matter in terms of the fundamental and primary. He said,

> Lao Tzu's book can almost be generalized into one phrase – to uphold the fundamental and lay to rest the incidental. (*A Brief Introduction to Lao Tzu*)

Wang Bi also proposed many important categories, such as:

1) Mother and children: "Mother is essential while children are incidental." (*Commentaries on Lao Tzu*, Chapter 52)

2) Essence and function: "Even those who have become very wealthy and come into possession of myriad things by dint of their outstanding virtue can only be virtuous in a separate sense, for though they may be commendable in choosing 'nothingness' as their function, they cannot do away with 'nothingness' in their essence." (Chapter 38)

3) Movement and stillness: "Though all things are moving, they will eventually return to void stillness, for that is the ultimate and genuine state of everything." (Chapter 16)

4) One and many: "The scarce are appreciated among the abundant; the minority is honored by the multitude." (*Brief Interpretations of Book of Change, Elucidating Tuan*)

Among these opposite categories, "mother," "essence," "one" and "stillness" are primary while "children," "function," "many" and "movement" are secondary.

This led to a change in the central concept of Dao. For Lao Tzu, Dao was the most basic concept, and "nothingness" was only an attribute of Dao. This was an inevitable consequence of his thoughts about origin. However, for Wang Bi the opposite became true, with "nothingness" being the more fundamental concept. He said,

**Dao is the name of nothingness. That which nothing can obstruct or bypass, we call it Dao.** (*Clarifying Doubts about the Analects*)

An assessment of this thought shows Wang Bi's superb analytical ability and outstanding skills at theoretical thinking. Thanks to these abilities he brought the understanding of Dao to a new ontological height. He also began to show a more distinct tendency toward idealism.

## Li

The second important concept relating to the issues of the origin and laws is "Li". It is connected, in some degree, to the concept of Dao.

The concept of Li appeared as early as in the pre-Qin period. For the very beginning, it was used to refer to the laws of things or nature. For instance:

Guan Zi said, "If someone goes against the Heavenly Way above and the Earthly Principle (*li*) below ..." (*Guan Zi, Explaining Situations*)

Chuang Tzu said, "As things were completed, there were produced the distinguishing lines (*li*) of each, which we call the bodily shape." (*Chuang Tzu, Heaven and Earth*)

Han Fei said, "Li means distinction between the square and the round, the short and the long, the coarse and the fine, and the hard and the fragile." (*Han Fei Zi, Explaining Lao Tzu*)

The time during which the concept of Li was developed (which happened during the Wei and Jin Dynasties (220-581), the Southern and Northern Dynasties (581-907), and the Sui and Tang Dynasties), should be regarded as an important period because of the wide application of the concept in science. For instance:

In astronomy, Du Yu said, "Days accumulate into months, months into years. During this process of the old giving way to the new, minute errors may occur, as dictated by the law (*li*) of nature." (*Book of Jin, Record of Calendars II*)

In mathematics, Zhao Shuang said, "Squares are regular, but circles are full of variations, making it necessary to devise methods for dealing with them (*li zhi*)." (*Commentaries on the Zhoubi Arithmetic Classic*)

In biology, Guo Pu said, "All things change, each following a different principle (*qi li wu fang*)." (*Comments on the Illustrated Edition of Er Ya, Clam*)

*Commentaries on the Water Classic*, a masterpiece of ancient Chinese geography, written by Li Daoyuan, during the Northern Wei Dynasty, and printed in the reign of Emperor Jiajing of Ming Dynasty.

In geography, Li Daoyuan said, "All things must change (*wu wu bu hua zhi li*)." (*Commentaries on the Water Classic, the Luo River*)

In medicine, Huangfu Mi said, "Diseases may worsen or abate, and acupuncture must vary in depth accordingly (*ge zhi qi li*) and never exceed the proper limit." (*ABC Classic of Acupuncture and Moxibustion*)

When discussing the theory of tides, Lu Zhao said, "That the sun sets into the sea must be a fixed law (*bi ran zhi li*)." (*Ode on Sea Tide*)

The term Li in all these quotations contains the meaning of "law." In later times, Liu Yuxi refined the concept in philosophical terms:

> **When a boat travels in the Wei River, the Zi, the Yi or the Luo, its speed and anchorage are controlled by the boatmen. A howling gale cannot raise billows, and the swirls of the stream cannot rise like mountains. Whether the boat goes fast and smoothly, or capsizes, or is stranded in the shallows, it would be the result of human action. Whatever happens, nobody in the boat would speak about the heaven, because they know the reason (*li*).**

> **When a boat travels in the Yangtze, the Yellow River, the Huai, or the Hai, no one can tell how fast it would go, or exactly where it could anchor. A wind that whistles through the boughs of trees could raise sun-eclipsing waves, and a small cloud the size of a carriage awning could produce curious events. Whether the boat sails safe and sound, or has the misfortune of sinking, or meets with danger but manages a narrow escape, it would be the result of the heaven's will. Whatever happens, nobody in the boat would speak about human action, because they do no know the reason (*li*). (*Treatise on Heaven II*)**

In these quotations Liu Yuxi not only discusses the relationship between heaven and the people of earth, but he also talks about the relationship between heaven and humans on the one hand and Li on the other. In particular, he thinks very deeply about laws. Such ruminations would become

a tradition that would be carried on by many thinkers of the Song Dynasty and of later times. For instance, Zhang Zai also regarded Li as law, saying, "There is Li in everything." (*Quotations from Zhang Zi II*)

It is noteworthy that, after the Qin and Han Dynasties, Chinese philosophy progressed from a consideration of Dao to a consideration of Li. The main reason for this was that, though both Dao and Li encompass the concept of laws or rules, they have different intellectual backgrounds or foundations. The concept of Dao mainly resulted from the development of astrology or astronomy during the pre-Qin period and derived from ideas about the Heavenly Way which had been developed by these disciplines. Unlike Dao, the concept of Li was related to the concept of generality from its very beginning. This meant that, as knowledge developed rapidly in the period after the Qin and Han Dynasties, Li was the concept that was most "fit for survival."

Finally, Li became a central concept of the neo-Confucianism developed by the Cheng brothers and, especially by Zhu Xi. Li then became a central concept of the Chinese philosophy of the late dynastic era. Take Zhu Xi's view for example. For him, Li mainly had the following meanings:

1) Origin or noumenon, as derived from the concept of Dao;

2) Laws or rules, also derived from Dao;

3) Ethics or morality.

The third meaning was, undoubtedly, based on a Confucian tradition, which can be traced back to the demarcation between "heavenly principles" and "human desires" in *Record on the Subject of Music in Book of Rites*.

The first meaning was particularly important because it concerned a major debate over the issue of Li versus Qi[12]. The Cheng brothers and Zhu Xi held clear opinions on this: in terms of sequence, Li precedes Qi, while, in terms of importance, Li is primary and Qi is secondary. Zhu Xi said,

---

12. For a discussion on the issue of principle and desire related to this point, see Chapter 3.

What existed before heaven and earth was, after all, nothing but Li. Thanks to the existence of Li, there are heaven and earth; if Li did not exist, there would be no heaven or earth, and no humans or everything else. Li gives rise to Qi, the circulation of which brings into existence everything in the world. (*Words of Zhu Zi, vol.1*)

Li is the metaphysical Dao, the origin of living things; Qi is a physical entity, responsible for the concrete forms of living things. (*Works of Zhu Wen Gong, vol. 58, Reply to Huang Daofu*)

It should be observed that Zhu Xi's consideration of the relationship between Li and Qi touches upon a fundamental issue in philosophy – the relationship between the general and the specific. In his opinion, it is impossible to keep tracing back specific things, which must originate from something not specific; conversely, generality would never only depend upon specific things and must have a reason for common existence. It should be understood that Zhu Xi was thinking deeply about one of the most fundamental issues in philosophy. However, by isolating the general from the specific, by believing that the former could exist apart from the latter and by thinking that it could even have an original, ontological status, he was bound to find his theory in a predicament. This is why Zhu Xi's philosophy is usually identified as "objective idealism".

## Qi

The third important concept that is related to discussions about the origin of the world is Qi.

The earliest philological explanation of the word Qi is found in Xu Shen's *Explanation on Chinese Characters*: "Qi ( 气 ) [pictographic]: cloud." Inspired by this definition, we can imagine that Qi could be formed by both natural and human activities, such as cloud, steam, heat from the firing of products, and smoke from the offering of sacrifices. The concept thus defined can be traced back to very early times, such as the New Stone Age. In other words, the concept of Qi came into existence much earlier than the word Qi, which was invented relatively late (this was because the concept of Qi was neither as substantial nor as useful as the Five Elements).

As early as in the Western Zhou Dynasty, attempts were made to use the concept of Qi to explain how things come into being and how they changed. This can be seen in Bo Yangfu's view on earthquakes and Yi He's discussion of diseases. The ideas of "two kinds of Qi" and "six kinds of Qi" became widespread during the Spring and Autumn Period, e.g.:

> **The six kinds of Qi are yin, yang, wind, rain, darkness, and brightness. (*The 1ˢᵗ Year of the Reign of Duke Zhao, Zuo Zhuan*)**

During the Warring States Period, the concept of Qi was very widely used, and many scholars and philosophical schools came to regard Qi as the origin of life and everything else in the universe. Guan Zi said, "The essence (of life) is what is essential to Qi." (*Guan Zi, Inner Business*) Chuang Tzu said, "Human life is a concentration of Qi. Concentration brings life, and dispersion results in death." (*Chuang Tzu, Knowledge Rambling in the North*)

The development of the idea of Qi reached a zenith during the Eastern Han Dynasty (25-220), when Wang Chong proposed his theory of primordial Qi (*yuanqi*). Specifically speaking, this theory contains the following ideas. First, everything in the world is generated by Qi – as Wang Chong put it,

Zhang Zai (1020-1077), a philosopher of the School of Mind from the North Song Dynasty, was born in Hengqu, Meixian County, Fengxiang (today Meixian County, Sha'anxi Province). He was also known as Mr. Hengqu. As he gave lectures in the central Sha'anxi Plain for a long time, his school was called Sha'anxi School.

All things are generated of their own accord when the Qi of Heaven and the Qi of Earth meet. (*Critical Essays, Nature*)

The genesis of everything depends on primordial Qi. (*On Toxins*)

Second, Qi is a natural thing. Wang Chong said, "Heaven and Earth are nature that contains Qi." (*Discourses on Heaven*) This also means that Qi has no consciousness.

Why is it that "heaven is natural and does nothing"? Because it is made up of Qi, which is simple and quiet, and devoid of desire, action or event. (*Nature*)

In emphasizing the natural property of Qi, Wang Chong was denying theological teleology. He also said,

All those which have blood and veins have life in them, and all living things will die – that is known for sure. Heaven and earth have no life, and therefore do not die; the same is true of yin and yang. (*The Void of Dao*)

That is to say that, as human and matter are concentrations of Qi they are as sure to die as they are to be born, whereas Qi exists forever, neither living nor dying, as a physical element. It can also be said that Wang Chong's theory of primordial Qi developed of the idea that Qi is the origin of the world to its most sophisticated level.

The idea of Qi developed to another peak during the Song Dynasty, when it made the transition from a theory of origin to an ontological theory. For hundreds of years afterwards, the ontological theory of Qi was gradually improved by a number of eminent scholars such as Zhang Zai and Wang Fuzhi.

Zhang Zai of the Northern Song Dynasty was the pioneer of the ontological theory of Qi. In his opinion, the entire world, which included both everything with forms and the formless "great void" (taixu), was unified in Qi. His thought boils down to the idea that the great void is Qi. He said,

**The Great Void cannot exist without Qi, which is bound to concentrate to form all things in the world, which in turn are bound to disperse into the Great Void.** (*Correcting the Unenlightened, The Supreme Harmony*)

**The Great Void, which is formless, is the noumenon of Qi. The concentration and dispersion of Qi are the objective manifestations of change.** (*ditto*)

As we can see, this ontological theory of Qi differs from the theory of Qi as the origin of the world in that it is not inclined toward the genesis of the universe; it also differs from the ontological theory of Dao or Li in that it emphasizes the materiality of the noumenon. In opposition to the views on void, nothingness and emptiness expressed in Buddhism and Taoism, Zhang Zai argued for the substantiality of the "great void" or Qi. As he put it:

**Knowing that the Great Void is made up of Qi, we know that there is no such thing as "nothingness."** (*ditto*)

As a physical entity, Zhang Zai thought that Qi could only concentrate or disperse, or be with or without form, with no distinction between life and death, or between existence and nonexistence. Additionally, Zhang Zai's discussions also contain the idea of the eternity of matter.

Since then, the ontological theory of Qi has been developed and improved by many thinkers, notably by Wang Fuzhi, who lived during the transition from the Ming to the Qing Dynasty (1368-1911). His improvements boil down to three ideas. His first idea was that Qi is spatially infinite. He said,

> Qi pervades the world, but it is so subtle and formless that we see void instead of Qi. (*Commentaries on Zhang Zai's Correcting the Unenlightened, The Supreme Harmony*)
>
> The yin Qi and the yang Qi permeate the Great Void, in which there is nothing else. (*ditto*)

Here "pervades the world" and "permeate the Great Void" are descriptions of infinity. What Wang Fuzhi did was to improve the ontological theory of Qi by leaving no room for anything beyond Qi, such as Dao or Li. Wang Fuzhi's second idea related to the views expressed by *Commentaries on Book of Change* and Zhu Xi on Dao vs. Qi and physical vs. metaphysical. He emphasized that "Dao means the Dao of Qi." (*External Commentaries on Book of Change, Xi Ci I*) This actually gives strong support to the theory of the supremacy of Qi. His third idea was about understanding Qi as something that was not concrete as much as possible. In this respect, Wang Fuzhi generalized the concept and took it onto a higher philosophical level, including within it categories such as "actual existence" (*shiyou*), "inherent existence" (*guyou*), and "sincerity" (*shi*). For example, he noted,

> Sincerity means actuality; actual existence means inherent existence. (*Elaborations on the Book of Documents, Great Plan III*)

The term "existence" as used here by Wang Fuzhi is of the same status and significance as the term "nothingness" in the ontological theory of Dao: both represent a high degree of abstraction.

# WHAT ARE THE RELATIONSHIPS BETWEEN THINGS?

The relationship between things was another important concern of the ancient Chinese philosophers. It was also another thing that made them different from their European counterparts. The ancient European philosophers were mainly concerned with the nature of things. Indeed, in one sense, European philosophy originated from the exploration of the question "What is the nature of it?" In China, however, it was quite different. In the history of Chinese philosophy, the commonest question was "What is the relationship between them?" In both ancient and modern China, the relationship between things has been a widely-discussed issue, one with which most philosophers have been involved with and discussed. This rarely happened in the history of European philosophy.

Chinese views on the relationships between things can be categorized into three main types, amongst ideas about the relationship between heaven and humans is the oldest. Indeed, this is likely to have been the earliest issue on which Chinese thinking about the relationship between things focused. It was notable that Chinese philosophers' thoughts on the concept of relationship had two outlooks, one dialectical and the other holistic, which between them presented the full essence of Chinese philosophy.

# The Relationship between Heaven and the Human, and its Religious and Intellectual Background

In ancient Chinese thought, the heaven-human relationship was very complex as it related to philosophical, religious and intellectual ideas. Religiously, it encompassed the concepts of Heaven-Human Harmony and Fate (*Ming*), with the latter concept also including the ideas of God's Will (*Tian Ming*) and Destiny (*Ming Yun*). Intellectually, it encompassed the theories of Heaven-Human Difference and Heaven-Human Rule, as well as the concepts of Properness (*Yi*), Dependence (*Yin*) and Force (*Li*).

## The Religious Approach to the Heaven-Human Relationship

In religion, the heaven-human relationship was originally thought of as the relationship between God and people. This idea can be traced back to as early as the Liangzhu Culture (about 5,000 years ago). A large number of jade ware items (like *Yu Bi* and *Yu Cong*) were unearthed in the ruins of the Liangzhu Culture. The following line in Rites of *Zhou Dynasty* (*Zhou Li*) suggests that these artefacts were used to worship the Heaven and the Earth: "The white jade (*Yu Bi*) is presented to worship the Heaven, while the yellow jade (*Yu Cong*) to worship the Earth." Zhang Guangzhi notes that the visual image of *Yu Cong* looks both round and square. More significantly, by connecting the round and square, *Yu Cong* symbolically associates the Earth with Heaven[13]. The symbolic meaning of *Yu Cong* can be demonstrated by looking at Chinese written characters. For instance, Guo Moruo observes that *shen* ( 申 ) pictographically looks like a thread that unites two things[14] (*Shen* can be translated as God, divinity, spirit or "spiritual power"). Yang Xiangkui further points out that these two things are actually the Heaven and Earth, and that *Shen* here functions as a medium[15]. In fact, the character *shen* ( 申 ) was, in all likelihood, based on the shape of *Yu Cong*.

The heaven-human relationship relies heavily on the idea Heaven-Human Harmony. In the civilized society, the idea Heaven-Human Harmony was presented by the Divine-right Theory of Kingship. For example, the *Book of Documents* (*Shang Shu*) recorded how Heaven punished humans:

"Youhu insulted the Five Elements and abandoned the calendar in Xia, Shang, and Zhou dynasties. Heaven deprived him of life." (*King Qi's Address at Gan*)

"Xia committed a crime. He feared the Heaven and corrected his mistake." (*King Qi's Address*)

"Now we were starting off. We must respect the Heaven and accept his punishment." (*King Wu's Address*)

The idea of Heaven-Human Harmony had a great impact on Chinese philosophers. This led to the development of the theories of Heaven-Human Response, Heaven-Human Connection, and Heaven-Human Affinity. These were proposed by Dong Zhongshu, a Han-Dynasty philosopher.

To Dong Zhongshu, the thing that made people human was Heaven (i.e. Heaven was the "great-grandfather" of all humanity). That was the reason why humans looked like the Heaven. For Dong Zhongshu, the form of the human body was predestined by Heaven, people's blood became benevolent by obeying Heaven's will, and people's virtue improved by following Heaven's law. People's likes or dislikes suggested Heaven's warmth or cold and people's joy or anger indicated

---

13. Zhang Guangzhi, *The Bronze Age of China*, Vol. 2. Beijing: SDX Joint Publishing Company, 1990, p. 71.

14. Guo Moruo, "A Study of Oracle Bone Inscriptions: Explanations to Heavenly Stems and Earthly Branches," cited in *Explanations to Ancient Chinese Characters*, Vol. 10. Shanghai: Shanghai Education Publishing House, 2004, p. 1148.

15. Yang Xiangkui, *A Study of Ancient Chinese Society and Thought*, Vol.1. Shanghai: Shanghai People's Publishing House, 1962, p. 162.

the winter or summer of the Heaven. In addition, people's fate materialized the four seasons of Heaven: Their joy, anger, sorrow, and happiness accorded with spring, autumn, winter, and summer. Joy, was therefore the symbol of spring, anger, the symbol of autumn, happiness, the symbol of summer and sorrow, the symbol of winter. Humans were the accessories of Heaven. These thoughts are found in *Luxuriant Dew of the Spring and Autumn Annals* [*Chun Qiu Fan Lu*], *The Heaven and Human*.

Dong Zhongshu also thought that Heaven had created the human body in the following way. It had been given 366 small condyles and 12 big condyles, to reflect the number of days and months in a year (a condyle is a prominence at the end of a bone). It had been given five internal organs, to reflect the Five Elements and four limbs, to reflect the four seasons. In addition, sight and blindness embodied day and night, hardness and softness represented winter and summer and sorrow and joy indicated *Yin* and *Yang*. People's plans and considerations resembled the Du-measure; and people's action and morality simulated the Heaven and Earth (this is the idea of *Heaven-Human Affinity*).

Undoubtedly, Dong Zhongshu's views seemed nonsensical and his theories were, later,

Jade wares *Yu Bi* and *Yu Cong* from the Warring States Period. These were unearthed in Zhangpan Town, Xuchang, Henan Province. They are part of the collection of the Henan Museum. *Cong* was a tubular jade ware that was used in sacrifice in ancient China. It was square outside and round inside. In ritual ceremonies, Bi was used to worship the heaven and Cong to worship the earth.

harshly criticized by Wang Chong. In *Critical Essays* (*Lun Heng*), Wang Chong refuted, "Confucius said the Heaven and Earth created humans consciously. This sounded groundless. The airflow in the Heaven and Earth assembled, and human was born occasionally. A man and woman satisfied their lust, and the child was born." (*The Law of Creatures*) He further declared that humans could not affect the heaven with their actions, neither did the Heaven. (*On the Pray for Rain*)

It must be noticed that for ancient Chinese philosophers the idea of Fate played an important part in the religious heaven-human relationship. This was because Fate was thought to be linked with God's Will and Destiny, both of which concerned the heaven-human relationship.

The link between the heaven-human relationship and God's will was an essential part of religious fatalism. In the Zhou Dynasty, for example, the core of religious fatalism was the Give-Accept relationship between Heaven and people, as this line in the *Book of Documents* (*Shang Shu*) suggests: "Hopefully, the King and his citizens undertook forever God's will," (*Duke Zhao's Memorial to the King*). In addition, people in the Zhou Dynasty developed the idea of being obedient to God's will: "Now that it was God's will, we must not defy it." (Sages) Later, these ideas spread to the Confucians. Confucius, for instance, viewed that a gentleman should fear and know God's will: "There were three things a gentleman must fear. The first one was God's will. A petty person showed no fear because he had no idea of God's will," (*The Analects, Ji Shi*). Confucius also commented on himself: "I understood God's Will at fifty," (*Wei Zheng*). In the *Doctrine of the Mean* (*Zhong Yong*), God's will was linked with human nature, morality, and education: "To respect human nature meant God's will, to follow human nature meant law, and to cultivate human nature meant education." Mysterious as these ideas on the heaven-human relationship may seem, they were commonly acknowledged by the Confucians.

The heaven-human relationship was also linked with the idea of Destiny, which also deals with the relationship between people and the external environment or the world. In ancient times, people attempted to understand or control their destinies through divination. In the discussions on divination in *Commentaries on Book of Change*, for instance, two divinatory symbols are mentioned – one for disaster and one for blessings in human's life. From these the idea of Destiny originated.

Confucians valued the idea of Destiny:

> **Life and death were decreed by Destiny; fortune and honor were determined by Heaven. (*The Analects, Yan Yuan*)**

> **The practice of law relied on Destiny; the abolition of law also relied on Destiny. (*The Analects, Xian Wen*)**

Here Confucius held the view that humans could not change things with their efforts, but that they must entrust themselves to Destiny. Similarly, Mencius asserted:

> **A person did what he was not asked as Destiny did; a person came although he was not required as Destiny did. (*Mencius, Wan Zhang II*)**

> **What mouth meant to taste was what eyes to form, what ears to sound, what nose to smell, the limbs to comfort. It was human's nature to like them, but it was Destiny that determined. Therefore, a gentleman seldom overstated human nature. (*Jin Xin II*)**

Here Mencius points out that, although liking comfort is part of human nature, whether a person obtains comfort or not depends on destiny. To Confucius and Mencius, Destiny was an aspect of God's will.

Chuang Tzu, a Taoist, also discussed Destiny:

> **Life or death, poverty or fortune, virtue or meanness, praise or slander, hunger or satiety, cold or warm, were all the results of change and the expression of Destiny. (*Chuang Tzu, Man's Spiritual World*)**

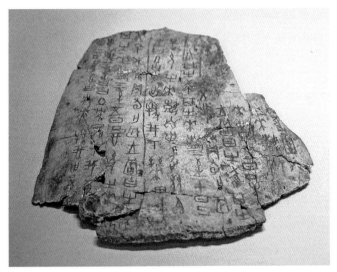

Animal bone used to practice divination, from during the reign of King Wuding of the Shang Dynasty. This was unearthed in Anyang, Henan Province. In around 1500 BC, diviners used animal's bone to predict the future. When the bone was cauterized, its back would crack. Then, diviners would foretell disaster or bliss based on the cracks that formed. The content and result of the divination were also inscribed on the bone.

To Chuang Tzu, a person displayed the most commendable conduct if he accepted predestined things calmly, (Conduct in Society). Chuang Tzu noticed that people could not "forget themselves" from the moment their bodies were formed to the moment they died. In *On the Similarity Between Things* he said that, no matter whether they contradicted or conformed with the external environment, people acted quickly "like a galloping horse". He thought that it was pitiful that nothing could stop them. He also noted that humans endured the misfortunes of their lives and did not know their destinies, and asked whether this sounded "woeful". Compared with Confucius and Mencius, Chuang Tzu took a more obviously fatalistic view.

The fatalistic view exerted enormous influence on philosophers in the Han Dynasty. Even Wang Chong, a great philosopher with a critical spirit, displayed strong fatalistic tendencies. Wang Chong remarked:

A person's life or death, poverty or fortune, were all determined by destiny. (*Critical Essays, On Fate and Fortune*)

**That a person encountered fortune meant he followed or disobeyed his destiny. He led a happy life if he encountered fortune, whereas he ended in misery if he encountered misfortune. (*Life*)**

Although Wang Chong discussed necessity and possibility, he failed to elaborate on the relationship between them. As a result, Wang Chong diminished the idea of Destiny and thought of it as an issue relating only to temperament and phrenology. He therefore drew the groundless conclusion that a person's destiny was decided by the Heaven and that it was presented in their appearance (which can be studied using phrenology, which considers the shape of the skull). To be fair, Wang Chong's understanding of the idea of Destiny was originally based on the principle of "following the heavenly law." However, due to the limitations of the period in which he lived, he fell into the trap of mysticism.

To conclude, the idea of Destiny has been a traditional concern of philosophers in China[16].

## The Intellectual Approach to the Heaven-Human Relationship

The intellectual or natural approach to the heaven-human relationship was examined by Chinese philosophers from two different perspectives.

The first related to (and was reliant on) objective laws, which were embodied in two important ideas, Properness (*Yi*) and Dependence (*Yin*).

The idea of Properness (*Yi*) developed from agricultural activities and consisted of two aspects: Properness in Time and Properness in Place. In the Xia and Shang dynasties, Properness in Time and Properness in Place were recorded in books such as the *Books of Calendar in Xia Dynasty (Xia Xiao Zheng)*, the *Canon of Yao* and *Tribute of Yu* of the *Book of Documents (Shang*

---

16. Evidently, the Chinese reliance on destiny differed from both the Western idea of relying on God and from the idea of "self-help." In fact, the Chinese's view on destiny is summed up in the phrases: "Man proposes; God disposes" and "Humans do their utmost and leave the rest to God's will." Both of which imply that people have the ability to act and not just to comply with destiny.

*Shu*) and the *Classic of Poetry* (*Sheng Min and Gong Liu*). In the Zhou Dynasty, the idea of Properness developed thanks to its practical use: "Properness in soil can be used to distinguish 12 constellations, tell the fortune or disaster that will befall a person's house, enrich people, confine birds and beasts, cultivate grass and wood, and benefit farming," (*Rites in Zhou Dynasty, Official of the Earth, Chief*). In the Spring and Autumn Period, the idea of Properness was developed further and improved. In the *Rites of Zhou Dynasty and Guan Zi*, Properness in Place was expounded upon and in *Guan Zi*, Properness in Place was discussed alongside the ideas of Category and Difference: "All herbs experience 12 months and then perish," (*On Earth*). Some ideas derived from the idea Properness in Time, such as According with Time, Complying with Time, and Considering the Situation. "A king should consider the situation and act in accordance with time, harmonize the Heaven and human and respect the natural law," (*Discourses of the States, The Discourse of Zhou II*). These ideas indicated the importance of following natural laws. The idea of Dependence (*Yin*) was also formed. This had a similar meaning to Properness (*Yi*). For instance, in the line, "The Heaven and Earth possess uniqueness," (*Zuo*

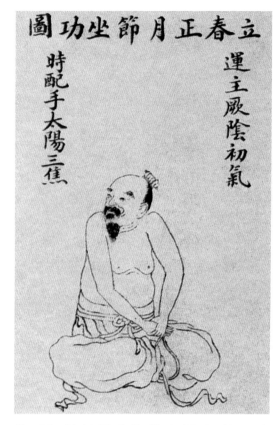

*Practicing Taoist Rite in the Start of Spring* (*January*), from "Medical Treatment by Practicing Taoist Rites in the Twenty-four Solar Terms". This was proposed by Chen Xiyi, a Taoist hermit in the early Song Dynasty. Chen Xiyi (871-989), whose literary name was Chen Tunan, was also called Chen Tuan or Fu Yao Zi. He was born in Boxian County, Anhui Province. To maintain health and cure disease, he created the "Medical Treatment by Practicing Taoist Rites in the Twenty-four Solar Terms". This was based on the correspondence between the flow of *Qi* in the Twenty-four Solar Terms and the meridian system of the human body.

*Zhuan, The 25<sup>th</sup> Year of the Reign of Duke Zhao*), the uniqueness of the Earth implied the necessity of Properness in Place. The idea Dependence (*Yin*), however, placed more stress on being obedient to natural law: "We must accept the disaster in nature," (*Discourses of the States, The Discourse of Yue II*). "To depend on the external environment," (*Guan Zi, Economic Plan*). As can be seen, a harmonious heaven-human relationship was thought of as being simple and direct. By the late Spring and Autumn Period, the idea of Properness (*Yi*) was no more confined to the heaven-human relationship. Rather, it extended to the military (Sun Tzu's use in war), to education (Confucius's use in education), to the political (Legalism's political theory), to the medicinal (the cure of disease in *The Inner Canon of the Yellow Emperor*), and to the philosophical (use in *Commentaries on Book of Change*). Later on, the idea Properness (*Yi*) played an important role in Chinese intellectual and ideological circles.

The second perspective from which the intellectual or natural approach to the heaven-human relationship was examined concerned the value of a person's spirit of initiative.

In the *Book of Documents* (*Shang Shu*), it was recorded that "People can undertake the Heaven's task," (*Gao Tao's Scheme*). Xun Zi was the earliest philosopher to clearly elucidate the human spirit of initiative. In his view, the heaven-human relationship concerned the difference between the heavenly and the human. He therefore wrote: "A man who can clarify the difference between the Heaven and human may be called a sage," (*Xun Zi, Treatise on Heaven*). The difference mentioned in this quotation refers to the difference between the duties of Heaven and the duties of people (with respect to objective laws or rules):

**If humans work hard on farming and reduce outgoing, the Heaven cannot impoverish them; if humans prepare reserve and respect the season, the Heaven cannot disease them; if humans follow the law and avoid deviation, the Heaven cannot bring them disaster... If humans abandon farming and pursue luxury, the Heaven cannot enrich them; if humans suffer deficiency and dislike farming, the Heaven cannot make them healthy; if humans violate the law and act wrong, the Heaven cannot bring them fortune. (*Treatise on Heaven*)**

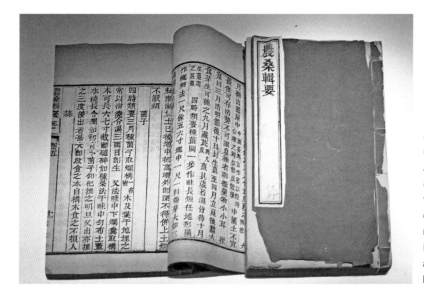

*Key Points in Agriculture* (*Nong Sang Ji Yao*), preserved by the National Museum of China. As a comprehensive book, it was complied by the Department of Agriculture in the early Yuan Dynasty and completed in 1273. It has seven volumes and includes knowledge on crop growing, sericiculture, livestock raising, fruit, wood and medicine. It summarizes developments in agricultural production in China before the Yuan Dynasty.

Meanwhile, Xun Zi recommended that people should display their spirit of initiative while respecting natural laws, as can be seen in the following passionate remark:

**Humans should master the natural law rather than worship Heaven; humans should use the natural law rather than admire Heaven; humans should control the natural law rather than expect from Heaven. Humans should exert their talent to expand farming rather than expect it to grow; humans should supervise things to maintain them rather than miss them after they are lost; humans should know the growing rule of things rather than hope for them to grow. Humans would never understand the law of things and use it if they make no effort and worshipped the Heaven. (*Treatise on Heaven*)**

Here Xun Zi cites six kinds of spirit relating to initiative. His famous assertion "to control and use the natural law" had a particularly profound influence on later philosophers. For instance, Liu Yuxi developed Xun Zi's theory into the Heaven-Human Rule.

It is important to note the value of a person's spirit of initiative with respect to intellectual activities, which was expressed by Chinese thinkers in the idea of Force (*Li*). The idea of Force (*Li*) countered the idea of Fate and refuted fatalism. In addition, the idea of Force negated the concept of Properness in Place and geomantic thought (geomancy is a type of divination) and contradicted the idea Properness (*Yi*). In some sense, the development of the ideas of a person's spirit of Initiative and of Force (*Li*) marked a great step forward, because it placed them in the context of intellectual rather than ideological activities.

As a matter of fact, human intellectual activities were valued as early as the Qin and Han dynasties. For example, in the *Book of Fan Shengzhi*, the method of furrow-titling (*Qu Zhong Fa*) was recorded.

In the Wei, Jin, Southern and Northern dynasties, the philosophical conflict between Force and Fate intensified, with the development of alchemy and the rise of Taoist theory. In *Bao Pu Zi*, Ge Hong (a Taoist during the Jin Dynasty) claimed that: "My fate is decided by myself not the Heaven. When the elixir is made, I will be immortal," (Vol. 1, *Huang Bai*, Cited from *Oracle Bone Inscriptions*). Without doubt, Ge Hong's view showed a pessimist outlook and challenged the traditional idea of Fate.

In the Song and Yuan dynasties, thanks to the development of gardening and horticulture, people had more varieties of plants to choose from. They therefore obtained a deeper understanding of the spirit of Initiative and Force.

**Humans' force benefits the growth of plant. (Han Yanzhi, *Records of Orange*)**

**Humans' force created masterpieces beyond the Heaven's power. (Wang Guan, *Peony in Yangzhou*)**

This understanding of people's Force had a significant impact on agricultural activity. As a result, in *Key Points in Agriculture* (*Nong Sang Ji Yao*), geomantic thought was denied. In the

Ming and Qing dynasties, the importance of human Force was further highlighted. For example, Lü Kun said, "It is certain that humans can conquer nature," (*Notes Taken while Reading* [*Shen Yin Yu Zhai*], Vol. 1). Lü Kun observed that in winter, "the flow of air was occluded, but in the old garden, flowers blossom and bear fruit." Lü Kun's view was shared by many thinkers:

**A plant adjusts to or disagrees with the soil. Humans exert or abandon force. Humans can conquer the Heaven if they use force, so can the soil. (Qiu Jun, *Supplementation to Commentaries of Great Learning*, Vol. 14)**

To know the time is the first, to know the soil is the second. Learning what Properness means first, and then taking the advantages and avoiding the disadvantages, human can conquer the Heaven with force. (Ma Yilong, *Knowledge on Agriculture*)

If the plant adjusts to the soil, it will not vary. (Xu Guangqi, *Encyclopedia of Agricultural Activities, Agriculture as the Root*)

If people observe the dryness and humidity and avoid the cold and heat, flowers will grow well. Even in the far and remote areas with different climates, humans' force can change flowers' living habits. (Chen Haozi, *On Growing Flower, On Growing Flower*)

Obviously, this deeper understanding of humans' force arose from advances in gardening, horticulture and agriculture, which confirms that intellectual progress in China contributed to ideological progress.[17]

In short, the idea of Force and its development provide us with an example which we can use to examine how philosophy impacts on science and how science deepens philosophy.

---

17. In addition, ideological activity, based on intellectual activity, was characterized by its realism and integrity, so it profoundly affected thinkers and philosophers. For instance, Zhang Xuecheng, a scholar during the Qing Dynasty, also held the view that humans could conquer nature (See *Theory on History*, *Tian Yu*). His view was certainly influenced by intellectual activity.

# The Dialectical Outlook

The dialectical outlook or dialectical thinking was one of the most remarkable achievements of ancient Chinese philosophy. Intellectually, this outlook was based on a study of opposite phenomena and it basically concerned the universal opposition amongst things. More specifically, the dialectical outlook was presented in three forms: mutual reliance, mutual transformation and the relativity of opposition. Using the dialectical outlook, Chinese thinkers treated things as a whole rather than as a part, considered things to be dynamic rather than static, and took a relativistic rather than an absolutist stance.

## Opposition

As mentioned in Chapter 1, the concept of opposition was similar in almost all nations, and in early philosophy it was acknowledged by philosophers in many different nations. However, the concept was only fully developed in China. The development of the concept of opposition in China should not be viewed as simply relating to an increase in the understanding of opposites. Instead, it should be viewed as the development of an abstracted or generalized view of opposition (the role of pictures and signs in this process has already been discussed).

Words with opposite meanings (antonym) appeared as early as the Shang and Zhou dynasties (1600-256 BC). There were examples of such words in the *Book of Documents* (*Shang Shu*) and the *Book of Change*. These included: left/right, early/late, up/down, big/small, hard/soft, fortune/ misfortune, comply/defy, go/come, light/heavy, even/slope, bliss/disaster, gentlemen/petty person, advance/retreat, exit/enter, heaven/earth, beginning/end, harm/benefit, presence/absence and self/ other. In the late Spring and Autumn Period, more such words emerged. In *The Art of War*, there

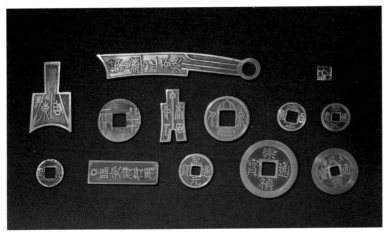

In Chinese philosophy, it was accepted that the heaven was round and that the earth was square. This concept was represented in ancient coins, which were round and had square holes. The form of such coins was established in the Qin Dynasty, and they were used until the Qing Dynasty (a period lasting more than 2,000 years).

were: death/life, live/die, *Yin/Yang*, winter/summer, far/near, difficult/easy, wide/narrow, reward/punish, win/lose, work/rest, many/few, advantage/disadvantage, big/small, strong/weak, go forward/go backward, up/down, other/self, attack/defend, sufficient/deficient, heaven/earth, odd/even, false/true, peace/disturbance, brave/timid, safety/danger, dynamic/static, round/square, stop/move, hunger/satiety, more/less, front/back, short/long, day/night, depart/meet, go/come, light/heavy, superior/inferior, hard/soft and contraction/expansion. In *Lao Tzu*, there were: presence/absence, big/small, up/down, early/late, long/short, light/heavy, host/guest, here/there, life/death, obverse/reverse, even/odd, good/bad, beautiful/ugly, disaster/bliss, superior/inferior, honor/shame, difficult/easy, advance/retreat, quiet/noisy, disadvantage/advantage, perfect/incomplete, wax/wane, success/failure, give/take, new/old, rise/fall, peace/disturbance, benefit/harm, open/close, breathe/inhale, start/end, bright/dark, curve/straight, hard/soft, strong/weak, wise/stupid, smart/clumsy, talkative/taciturn, past/present, full/empty and Yin/Yang. In *Commentaries on Book of Change*, there were: *Yin/Yang*, hard/soft, full/empty, go/come, winter/summer, inner/outer, increase/decrease, superior/inferior, up/down, noble/humble, advance/retreat, heaven/earth, *Qian/Kun*, motion/quiescence, man/woman, husband/wife, gentleman/petty person, fortune/misfortune, day/night, water/fire, start/end, death/life, safety/danger, rise/fall, live/die, gain/lose, odd/even, little/few, depart/meet, easy/difficult, contraction/expansion, harm/benefit, static/dynamic, eternal/changing, sufficient/deficient,

The Chinese idiom that "One's spear contradicts one's shield" is an example of a typical opposition. In *Han Fei Zi*, it is recorded that: A man sold both spear and shield, saying his spear and shield were the best. However, he was silent when others asked "How about stabbing the shield with the spear?"

bliss/disaster, increase/decrease and done/doing. The idea Opposition also affected science, especially medicine. In *The Inner Canon of the Yellow Emperor*, there were: *Yin/Yang*, heaven/ earth, man/woman, heaven/human, up/down, left/right, for/against, hard/tender, clear/dirty, motion/ quiescence, root/branch, slow/quick, phenomenon/nature, thick/thin, come/go, front/back, heat/ cold, water/fire, dry/wet, warm/cool, life/death, rise/fall, slow/urgent, empty/full, exit/enter, many/ few, here/there, absorb/excrete, success/failure, good/bad, start/end, joy/anger, profit/justice, deep/ shallow, thick/thin, greet/leave, fortune/misfortune, skew/straight and dynamic/static.

It is notable that the idea of Opposition was presented in the form of opposite concepts. The wide range and use of these opposite concepts established solid foundations for the development of the idea itself. In the Spring and Autumn Period, the highly abstract ideas "Liang" and "Er" (both of which mean "two") appeared. They are illustrated in the following quotation: "Everything has two sides… The body has a left and right. The superior corresponds to the inferior. King to duke, vassal to official. All present in the form of two," *(Zuo Zhuan, The 32$^{nd}$ Year of the Reign of Duke Zhao)*.

**Everything has *Yin* and *Yang* sides. (*Lao Tzu*, Chapter 42)**

Tao means *Yin* and *Yang*. (*Commentaries on Book of Change, Xi Ci I*)

Divinity means the mystery of *Yin* and *Yang*. (*Commentaries on Book of Change, Xi Ci I*)

The wide use of the concept of *Yin-Yang* facilitated the expression and communication of thoughts about opposites. In addition, the concept of what we now call "contradictions" (*Mao Dun*) began to emerge. As can be seen from the following quotation: "It is impossible that a shield can resist all spears and a spear can penetrate all shields." (*Han Fei Zi, Difficulty in Unification*). These thoughts from Pre-Qin times laid the foundation for the development of the idea of Opposition:

Things cannot exist without their contradictories. (Zhang Zai, *Correcting the Unenlightened, Animal*)

Things appear in couples. *Yin* must with *Yang*, *Yang* must with *Yin*. (Zhu Xi, *Words of Zhu Zi*, Vol. 95)

To conclude, the idea Opposition has been an important element in the history of Chinese philosophy.

## Mutual Reliance

To elaborate on the dialectical outlook, it is necessary to examine mutual reliance among things. This idea was fully considered by Lao Tzu, who believed that two opposites co-exist and supplement each other:

> **Presence and absence appear and contradict, difficult and easy form and contradict, long and short present and contradict, high and low foil and contradict, sound and tone harmonize and contradict, and front and back follow and contradict. (*Lao Tzu*, Chapter 2)**

Here, Lao Tzu highlighted the universality of the idea of Opposition using examples. He also noted that human life was the same:

> **If people all view the beauty as beauty, then it turns to be ugliness; if people all see the kindness as kindness, then it turns to be vice. (*Lao Tzu*, Chapter 2)**

> **The virtuous man can be the teacher for the wicked man; the wicked man can be the lesson to the virtuous man. (Chapter 27)**

Yin-Yang (*Taiji*), illustrates the mutual generation and mutual overcoming of *Yin* and *Yang*.

For Lao Tzu this meant that beauty and ugliness co-existed, even though they contradicted each other. The same was true for and kindness and vice. In the same way, he thought that knowing beauty meant knowing ugliness, and that knowing kindness meant knowing vice. Lao Tzu also noted that when opposition was obvious, people would recognize it, but that when it was obscure, people would neglect it. For instance, on harm and benefit, disaster and bliss, Lao Tzu said,

> **What harms may benefit; what benefits may harm. (Chapter 42)**

> **Disaster, that is where bliss depends; bliss, that is where disaster underlies. (Chapter 58)**

It can be clearly seen that Lao Tzu not only discussed objective phenomena, but also advocated a way of thinking: that the idea of Opposition was ubiquitous and that people should therefore always bear it in mind.

In a similar way to *Lao Tzu*, the *Commentaries on Book of Change* also stressed the co-existence and complementary nature of opposites:

> **The Heaven is superior and the Earth is inferior, stabilizing the positions of Hexagram *Qian* and Hexagram *Kun*. With the superior and inferior presented, all lie in their positions. The movement of the Heaven and the quiescence of the Earth accord with the law, clarifying hard (*Gang*) and soft (*Rou*). (*Xi Ci I*)**

Unlike *Lao Tzu*, *Commentaries on Book of Change* emphasized the interaction of opposites:

> **The hard (*Gang*) and soft (*Rou*) interact (*Mo*), and the Eight Diagrams forms (Dang). (*Xi Ci I*)**

> **The hard (*Gang*) and soft (*Rou*) interfere (*Tui*), and changes happen. (*Xi Ci I*)**

Here, "interact" (*Mo*), "form" (*Dang*), and "interfere" (*Tui*) referred to the interaction of the opposites. The *Commentaries on Book of Change* also conveyed another important view – that the existence of things was based on their opposites rather than things they are related to. This view was similar to the idea of *He Shi Sheng Wu* (the harmonized existence breeds things) proposed by Shi Bo. The difference lies in the fact that Shi Bo emphasized variety while *Commentaries on Book of Change* stressed opposition. This can be seen by looking at the two Hexagram *Kui* and Hexagram *Ge* diagrams. Hexagram *Kui* lies above Hexagram *Dui* and below Hexagram *Li*, and Hexagram *Ge* lies above Hexagram *Li* and below Hexagram *Dui*. Hexagram *Li* means woman in the middle, and Hexagram *Dui* means woman below. Therefore, Hexagram *Li* and Hexagram *Ge* can both be interpreted as "two women living together." According to the *Commentaries on Book of Change*, "Two women living together will not act in agreement, (*Hexagram Kui, Tuan Zhuan*), and "If two women live together, they think differently. (*Hexagram Ge, Tuan Zhuan*). This indicates that the two women were related conceptually to each other and that, as a result they excluded each other and could not be harmonized. Indeed, the *Commentaries on Book of Change* maintained that it was different or opposite things that constituted harmony and that difference or opposition was the precondition of harmony: "The Heaven and the Earth differ but serve the same; man and woman differ but think the same; things vary but express the same," (Hexagram Kui, *Tuan Zhuan*). The idea embodied in *Commentaries on Book of Change* was profound, and was consistent with Hegel's thought: "Thing excludes what are akin to it and identifies what are different from it."[18] In addition, the *Commentaries on Book of Change* acknowledged the primary and secondary status of the opposites: "The Heaven is superior and the Earth is inferior." This indicates that human's understanding had been deepened. However, in the *Commentaries on Book of Change,* everything that was masculine and hard was classified into the Hexagram *Qian* (and therefore classed as superior), and all that was feminine and soft was classified into the Hexagram *Kun* (and therefore classed as inferior). Obviously, this division conformed to a certain pre-existing rule and consolidated the superior-inferior relationship. It therefore fell into the trap of essentialist thinking.

Afterward, philosophers of the Song and Ming dynasties deepened their understanding of the

---

18. G. W. Hegel, *Phenomenology of Spirit*, Vol. 1. Beijing: Commercial Press, 1979, p. 106.

ideas of Opposition and Harmony on the basis of *Lao Tzu* and the *Commentaries on Book of Change*:

There is no harmony without the existence of the opposites; there is no opposite without the existence of harmony. (Zhang Zai, *Correcting the Unenlightened, The Supreme Harmony*)

The harmony can exist if the opposites are present; the harmony cannot exist if the opposites are absent. (Zhu Xi, *Words of Zhu Zi*, Vol. 98)

A thing cannot exist without its opposite. A thing and its opposite exist in harmony. (Fang Yizhi, *Dong Xi Jun, Fan Yin*)

Two things that co-exist are in fact two opposites. (Wang Fuzhi, *External Commentaries on Book of Change, Xi Ci I*)

These thoughts further developed the ideas of Opposition and Mutual Reliance.

# Transformation

Transformation is another important idea in dialectical thinking.

People's concerns about the idea of Transformation (as with many of the concepts described above) developed from the observations they made of nature: the change from hotness to coldness and winter to spring, the rise and fall of the sun and the wax and wane of the moon. The idea of Transformation was firstly recorded in the *Book of Change*, in which Hexagram *Tai* and Hexagram *Pi* embodied the transformation of opposites. This is described in lines such as: "The large comes when the small leaves." "The small comes when the large leaves." "There will be no slope without even." "There will be no return without departure." and "Fortune follows after disaster."

During the Spring and Autumn Period, the idea of Transformation was widely acknowledged and discussed by many philosophers:

Cai Mo [Shi Mo] cited the line from the *Classic of Poetry*: "A high bank can be called valley,

and a deep valley can be called hill," (*Zuo Zhuan, The 32<sup>nd</sup> Year of the Reign of Duke Zhao*).

Another aspect of transformation was highlighted by Guan Zi:

"Love is the start of hate; good is the source of evil," (Guan Zi, *Guan Zi, On Tao*).

These opinions suggest that philosophers in the Spring and Autumn Period had realized that the opposites of things were contained in the things themselves. In the late Spring and Autumn Period, Sun Tzu extended the idea of Transformation to the military field: "The disturbance comes from the peace, the timidity from the valor, and the weakness from the strength," (*The Art of War, Energy*). More importantly, Sun Tzu noticed the military use of the idea of Transformation and showed how disadvantage could be transformed to advantage:

"Only when put in danger can soldiers turn danger to safety; only when put in peril can soldiers turn peril to hope," (*The Nine Situations*).

He also noted that an enemy's advantage could be turned into their disadvantage:

For the enemy, the comfort can tire them, the satiety can hunger them, and the rest can disturb Them. (*The False and the Real*).

During the time Sun Tzu was writing, the idea of Transformation was viewed as an approach of great significance. It was thought to confirm the authenticity of dialectics. It therefore constituted a prominent feature of Chinese philosophy.

However, it was Lao Tzu who endowed the idea of Transformation with true philosophical meaning. Based on his wide observations and deep thinking, Lao Tzu discovered the universality of Transformation:

**What seems natural may seem strange; what looks good may seems evil. (*Lao Tzu*, Chapter 58)**

**The army that seems too invincible may lose; the tree that seems too hard may break. (Chapter 76)**

**The movement of Tao means the endless transformation of the opposites. (Chapter 40)**

**Things will decline when they have reached their full development. (Chapter 55)**

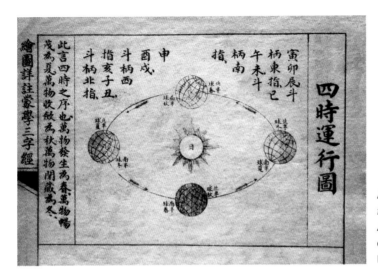

An illustration in *Three Character Classic for Children Learning with Illustrations: The Alternation of the Four Seasons*. This was drawn by Jinzhang Bookstore in the early Republic of China.

Lao Tzu realized that things will develop in the opposite direction when they become extreme and that this was an eternal law in nature. These famous remarks have come to symbolize the wisdom not only of Lao Tzu's philosophy but of all Chinese philosophy.

Lao Tzu also considered the application of the idea of Transformation, and his thoughts embodied more philosophical color than Sun Tzu. Lao Tzu proposed two paradigms for transformation.

The first related to the promotion of transformation: "To contract one thing, man must first expand it; to weaken one thing, man must first strengthen it; to abolish one thing, man must first popularize it; to seize one thing, man must first abandon it," (Chapter 36).

The second related to the deferment of transformation: "Man can make himself safe if he compromises; branch can make itself straight if it bends. Emptiness will turn to fullness; oldness will turn to newness. Man can obtain more if he hopes less; man can delude himself if he hopes more," (Chapter 22).

We must admire Lao Tzu's wisdom. Of course, it is also the wisdom of the Chinese.

In the Warring States period, the *Commentaries on Book of Change* developed the idea Transformation to a new stage. Like Lao Tzu, the *Commentaries on Book of Change* also believed that transformation was common and that it was a circular process:

> **The moon rises when the sun falls and the sun rises when the moon falls; the alternate of the sun and moon creates the day. Summer comes when winter leaves and winter comes when summer leaves; the change of winter and summer forms the year. (*Xi Ci II*)**

> **To open and close forms the change; to come and leave incessantly means fluency. (*Xi Ci I*)**

Lao Tzu's idea of Transformation led to the conclusion that things are circular. At the same time, the *Commentaries on Book of Change* observed that transformation commenced when things became extreme: "Man should change when he is at the end of his tether, as to change will result in new direction and new direction will result in long," (*Xi Ci II*).

However, the *Commentaries on Book of Change* and *Lao Tzu* suggested different responses to the reality of transformation. Generally speaking, Lao Tzu recommended that things should seem weak to avoid or defer transformation, whereas the *Commentaries on Book of Change* stressed the hard (*Gang*) side of things. To defer transformation, the *Commentaries on Book of Change* suggested that man should be prepared for danger in times of safety: "A gentleman should remind himself of the danger when in safety, of fall when in rise, and of disturbance when in peace," (*Xi Ci II*). It also recommended that man should discard the old and favor the new and always reform himself: "To learn the nature means great accomplishment; to progress every day means great virtue; and to change ceaselessly means *Yi*," (*Xi Ci II*).

As mentioned above, ancient Chinese philosophers had had deep thoughts on the idea of Transformation as early as the Sping and Autumn and Warring States periods. They dealt with both objective laws and subjective methods, and therefore developed the idea of Transformation to a high level. The idea of Transformation was discussed elsewhere in the history of Chinese philosophy. For instance, Cheng Yi claimed, "Things will turn to the opposite when they reach the extreme," (*Cheng's Notes on Commentaries on Book of Change*, Vol.1). While Zhu Xi said, "When the line moves from the Yin to Yang or from Yang to Yin, man should advance or retreat," (*Words of Zhu Zi*, Vol. 74).

## Relativity

When philosophers had obtained a full understanding of the idea of Opposition, they would begin to speculate: was Opposition an absolute or a relative idea? The answer to this question was, without doubt, an important part of the dialectical outlook.

Lao Tzu realized the relative nature of the idea of Opposition. He noted that things that seemed opposite were surprisingly alike:

> The clear road seems obscure; the road that leads to the front seems to the back; the smooth road seems rough. The lofty seems low; the honest seems dishonest; the sufficient seems deficient; the strong seems weak; the simple seems cunning; the most rectangular seems edgeless. The great mind matures slowly; the large bell sounds silent; the obvious image seems invisible. (*Lao Tzu*, Chapter 41)

> The perfect seems flawed but cannot be exhausted; the fullest seems empty but cannot be used up; the straightest seems curved; the smartest seems clumsy; the most eloquent seems taciturn. (Chapter 45)

Here Lao Tzu tells us that Opposition is not an absolute idea. In addition, Lao Tzu refuted the "either-or" way of thinking. This more flexible approach embodied great creativity and enormously influenced Chinese philosophy.

One obvious example was the relativism proposed by Chuang Tzu. His ideas about relativism originated from Lao Tzu's thoughts, however, he overstated the similarity between things while

denying their differences, and drew some inaccurate conclusions. However, to be fair, some of his views were rational. For instance, he observed that the ideas of Difference and Opposition were not absolute, and that beneath opposite things or phenomena lay the similarities between them.

"When man mentions the difference, he will see that all are large if he sees largeness and that all are small if he sees smallness.

"When man mentions function, he will see that all have function if one thing has and that none have function if one thing does not.

"When man mentions judgment, he will consider that all are right if he affirms the thing and consider that all are wrong if he denies the thing.

"However, viewed from Tao, there was nothing superior or inferior," (*Chuang Tzu, Qiu Shui*). Here Chuang Tzu is saying that opposite things or phenomena (e.g. large/small, presence/absence, right/wrong) all share a certain similarity. Therefore, a person should notice the similarity between things or phenomena when he or she discovers their opposition or difference.

In *On the Similarity between Things*, Chuang Tzu expounded on this theme of the similarity between things:

**All contain what are opposite to them; all contain what are similar to them.**

**All live when they die and all die when they live; all turn to be right when they are wrong and all to be wrong when right.**

**One side of the thing is also the other of it, and vice versa. There is right and wrong both in one side and the other. Is there one thing that contains opposite sides? Is there one thing that does not contain opposite sides? That there is an absolute opposite side in one thing is the core of *Tao*.**

**Things contain what are considered right and what are recognized. There is nothing that does not contain the right side and nothing that cannot be recognized. Take the thin stem and high column, the ugly and beautiful, as an example. Although they vary in size and appearance, they are the same in *Tao*. Things form when they decay and decay when form. In *Tao*'s view, thing's**

*Dreaming of Butterfly* (Part), drawn by Liu Guandao during the Yuan Dynasty. This picture was inspired by a dream that had been recounted by Chuang Tzu. Using his romantic imagination and flowery language, Chuang Tzu described his transformation into a butterfly in the dream and the butterfly's transformation into him after the dream. He proposed the views that one could not clearly distinguish the real from the unreal or life from death.

**formation and decay are not different.**

Chuang Tzu equated Qi Wu with "One" and "Same". He also considered "the opposite as the core of Tao." As a result, Chuang Tzu ignored the difference and opposition between things. He developed the idea of Relativity into Relativism and developed Relativism into Absolutism, contradicting the dialectics based on the idea of Opposition. Nevertheless, Chuang Tzu's *Qi Wu* theory cannot be reduced to the relativistic view.

Chuang Tzu said, "The Heaven and the Earth co-exist with me, and all are harmonious with me," (*On the Similarity between Things*).

In his thoughts Chuang Tzu revealed his broad, calm and leisured mind, profound wisdom, wide optimism and deep tolerance. He also showed that he had eliminated prejudice and selfishness and revealed his deep understanding of the relationships between people and heaven and people and the outer world. In some sense, Chuang Tzu's view accorded with Zhang Zai's claim that, "People, my compatriot; nature, my congener."

# The Holistic Outlook

The holistic outlook was an important idea in ancient Chinese philosophy. It developed from the ideas of Opposition and Symmetry. Specifically, the holistic outlook had four main aspects: the "golden mean," the "consideration of both sides," "synthesis" and "association." Together, these explained the holistic outlook and its practical value. Comparatively speaking, there was no similar philosophical approach in ancient Greek or even ancient European philosophy.

## The Golden Mean

The concept of the Golden Mean was also known as "neutral," "middle" or "impartial." In today's terminology, it means balanced, proportionate, or moderate. The concept puts forward the idea that at all things or actions contain two corresponding or opposite sides, and that things or actions look rational/irrational or perfect/imperfect if their two sides are in/out of balance. Obviously, the idea of the Golden Mean was originally based on symmetry and the idea of Opposition.

The idea of the Golden Mean was first recorded in the *Canon of Yao of Book of Documents* (*Shang Shu*): "A man is supposed to be righteous and gentle, generous and earnest, strong and humane, and austere and honest." The concept was also called "Nine Virtues" (*Jiu De*) in *Gao Tao's Scheme*: "A man should be generous and earnest, gentle and insightful, honest and respectful, capable and careful, calm and resolute, righteous and gentle, austere and clean, powerful and prudent, and valiant and faithful." It can therefore be assumed that the idea of the Golden Mean  originally related to human's virtue. It was Confucius who developed the idea. Confucius concentrated on the role that the concept played in the cultivation of morality, namely the rationality

and perfection of behavior. Confucius discussed the concept in a number of different ways:

"Both-And" Sentence, both confirmed: The Confucius is gentle and righteous, stately and respectful and graceful and calm. (*The Analects, Shu Er*).

"Not-But" Sentence, one confirmed: The poem "Crying Ospreys" sounds joyful but not indecent, sorrowful but not deplorable, (*Ba Yi*); the gentleman stresses harmony but not sameness; the gentleman remains poised but not arrogant, (*Zi Lu*).

Here "Joyful, " "sorrowful," "harmony ," and "poised' were moderate in nature, while "indecent," "deplorable," "saneness," and "arrogant" were biased.

Confucius also discussed what things violated the idea of the Golden Mean: "Excess is just as bad as deficiency," (*Xian Jin*).

The idea of the Golden Mean was later inherited by Confucians. For instance, in the Doctrine of the Mean (*Zhong Yong*), it was said,

**The honest man never compels himself to act decent and think right. A man who fulfills the idea of Golden Mean can be a sage.**

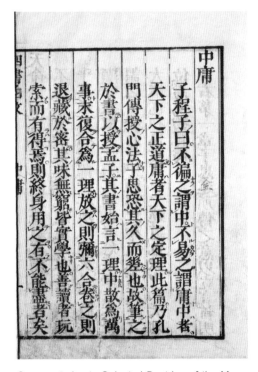

*Commentaries to Selected Doctrine of the Mean*, an ancient Chinese book, printed in the reign of Emperor Meiji in Japan.

Stone tablets with inscriptions that read: "Mencius' Mother Stopping Weaving," "Mencius' Mother Transferring Home Three Times," and "Zi Si Writing *Doctrine of the Mean*". They are in the Mencius Temple in Zoucheng, Shandong Province. It was said that the *Doctrine of the Mean* was composed by Zi Si. Zi Si (483-402 BC), also known as Kong Ji, who was the lineal grandson of Confucius. He was educated by Zeng Sen, an eminent student of Confucius. Confucius' doctrine was handed down from Zeng Sen to Zi Si, then from Zi Si's student to Mencius.

The idea Golden Mean is the foundation of a country.

He masters both excess and deficiency and rules the country with Golden Mean[19].

The idea of the Golden Mean or Balance was presented in a concrete form in ancient Chinese medicine, especially in *The Inner Canon of the Yellow Emperor*. According to *The Inner Canon of the Yellow Emperor*, the human body consisted of *Yin* and *Yang*. In general, it was thought that a person would have good health when their *Yin* and *Yang* were balanced: "When *Yin* and *Yang* are balanced, a man presents good complexion and sanguinity. When the pulses in nine places are harmonious, a man is healthy," (*Basic Questions, On Controlling the Meridian System*). However, as human life was affected by internal and external factors, traditional Chinese doctors thought that *Yin* and *Yang* rose and fell and always changed. They thought that, when the balance between *Yin* and *Yang* was broken, a person would develop a disease:

---

19. It was acknowledged that Aristotle, a Greek philosopher, also valued the idea of the Golden Mean.

When *Yang* exceeds *Yin*, a person's pulse flows quickly and they becomes dysphoric; when *Yin* exceeds *Yang*, a person's five organs and blood disharmonize each other and the person becomes pale. (*On Human's Vitality*)

When *Yin* exceeds, *Yang* is impaired and a person feels cold; when *Yang* exceeds, *Yin* is impaired and the person feels warm. (*On Yin and Yang*)

*The Inner Canon of the Yellow Emperor* suggested many ways to re-establish Yin-Yang balance: "Make a person warm when he feels cold and make him cold when he feels warm." "Contract when expansion happens and expand when contraction happens." "Supplement when a person feels feeble and excrete when a person feels full." (*On Disease and Climate*)

In addition, in *The Inner Canon of the Yellow Emperor*, the concepts of "sufficiency" and "deficiency" were used. These allowed people to understand in a visual way the imbalance and balance of *Yin* and *Yang*: "Excrete when a person feels sufficient and supplement when they feel deficient," (*On Controlling the Meridian System*). In short, the book said that a person must maintain the balance of their *Yin* and *Yang* in order to keep healthy. This was the fundamental concept put forward in *The Inner Canon of the Yellow Emperor* and is arguably the most profound piece of wisdom to have emerged from ancient Chinese medicine.

## Consideration of Both Sides

The idea of the Consideration of Both Sides ("Jian" or "Jian Liang") was influenced by the concepts of the Golden Mean and of Balance. It meant that, in any matter, two opposite sides should be taken into account, rather than one. This idea was developed to assure completeness and avoid one-sidedness.

The idea of the Consideration of Both Sides appeared as early as the Spring and Autumn Period. In *The Analects*, Confucius told his disciples, "A man with less knowledge asked me, but I did not know the answer. Then, I enlightened him by asking the two opposite sides of his question,"

Wei Zheng (580-643) was a renowned official in early Tang Dynasty and famous for admonishing the emperor. One of his well known remarks was, "A person will be enlightened if he listens to more voices and be fooled if he listens to less voices."

(*Zi Han*). In this instance, although Confucius did not have the specific knowledge needed to directly answer a question, he was able to help solve it by considering it from two opposite sides. This idea was also applied in military theory. In *The Art of War*, Sun Tzu stressed the necessity of considering both sides, "A wise general must take the advantage and disadvantage into account when he is deciding," (*The Nine Changes*). In the middle and late Warring States Period, the idea was widely accepted amongst the Chinese and was used to observe, analyze and judge things. For instance, in the *Commentaries on Book of Change*, one-sided thinking was criticized:

> **Should a man be called a sage, who knows advance but not retreat, life but not death, and gain but not loss? (*Hexagram Qian, Wen Yan*)**

While the way of thinking that considered both sides was affirmed and advocated:

> **A gentleman should remind himself of the danger when in safety, of fall when in rise, and of disturbance when in peace." (*Xi Ci I*)**

> **A man who knows the obscure and clear, the soft (*Rou*) and hard (*Gang*), can be respected by others." (*Xi Ci I*)**

The idea was also embodied in agricultural and medical activities. In *The Annals of Lü Buwei*, it was recorded, "The rule for farming is as follows. To make the hard soil soft and the soft soil hard. To farm the unused land and fallow the seeded. To fertilize the barren land and sterilize the fertile. To loosen the solid soil and stabilize the loose. To dry the wet soil and wet the dry," (*Making Use of the Earth*). In *The Inner Canon of the Yellow Emperor*, it says, "A man who is skilled in using a thin needle should insert into the *Yin* point to lead the *Qi* in the *Yang* point and into the *Yang* point to lead the *Qi* in the *Yin* point, into the left point to cure the disease in the right and into the right to cure the disease in the left," (*Basic Questions, On Yin and Yang*).

Philosophically, Xun Zi elaborated on the idea of the Consideration of Both Sides in the deepest way. Xun Zi criticized one-sided thinking, "When people see what they desire, they forget what they dislike; when people see what benefits them, they neglect what harms them," (*Xun Zi, Being Earnest*). He certainly considered one-sided thinking or one-sided understanding to be harmful. To avoid it, he stated that a person should consider both sides of an issue, rather than one side, while judging things, "When a person sees what they desire, they should remember what they dislike; when a person sees what benefits them, they should consider what harms them," (*Xun Zi, Being Earnest*). Xun Zi defined this "considering-both-sides" approach to thinking as *Jian* (Both):

> **People should count both sides and consider carefully before they decide what they desire or dislike, take or abandon, by which they will make less mistakes. (*Xun Zi, Being Earnest*)**

> **People should list both sides and make a criterion, so that the different things cannot be confused or disordered. (*Removing Obstructions*)**

Here, Xun Zi meant that a person should view a question as a whole, or consider both its sides, to ensure that they analyze or judge it correctly. At the same time, he saw "considering-both-sides" thinking as key to a ruler's success or failure: "A ruler who knows all happening in his country and has time to correct mistakes masters the most effective way to rule," (*Ruling the Country*). "A ruler who respects and follows other's opinion will obtain all citizens' support," (*The Law for Rule*). Xun Zi's thoughts had a great impact on later philosophers.

## Synthesis

The idea of the Consideration of Both Sides advocated a dichotomous approach to addressing a problem. In fact, the ancient Chinese considered questions to be multifaceted while solving them. Today we call this approach Synthesis ("Can," "He," or "Can He"), which features a consideration of all-sides of a problem or issue.

As a way of thinking, the idea of Synthesis was first used in the military field. In *The Art of War*, Sun Tzu said, "In the war, one should compare the conditions of both parties to judge who will win based on the five aspects. One is *Tao* (citizen's support), two is *Tian* (climate), three is *Di* (geographic condition), four is *Jiang* (general), and five is *Fa* (discipline). All are well known to generals. One who masters them shall win and who does not shall lose. In addition, man should consider the details of the five aspects to decide who will win. Whose ruler is wiser? Whose general is more talented? Whose geographic condition is more favorable? Whose rule is practiced more effectively? Whose soldiers are stronger? Whose soldiers are better trained? Who rewards and punishes in a just way? Then, he can know who will win," (*Plan Before the War*). Here, Sun Tzu analyzed the military condition by viewing it as a whole. That is, Sun Tzu considered war to be a rivalry between synthesized factors rather than a confrontation that simply pitted the antagonists against each other. Later, Han Fei developed the idea of Synthesis and put it into practice. To Han Fei, the idea of Synthesis (*Can*) led to the action of Synthesizing (*Can Wu*):

> **One can testify whether an opinion is true or false by synthesizing all the factors (Can Wu).** (***Han Fei Zi, Be Alert on the Intimate Ministers***)
>
> **To testify things by comparing it with others; to find the weakness by synthesizing all the factors.** (***Enhancement of the Ruler's Power***)

By *Can Wu*, Han Fei meant that one should take all the factors of a problem or issue into account and compare them. At the core of this approach was the idea that one must view the

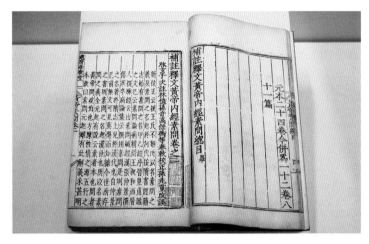

"Central Area" and "Basic Questions," printed in Ming Dynasty, and part of the collection of the National Museum of China. "Central Area" and "Basic Questions" constituted *The Inner Canon of the Yellow Emperor*, which was the first systematic medical work in China. It summarized medical experiences from before the Qin and Han dynasties and proposed the theories of *Zang-Fu*, the meridian system, and pathogenesis. It established the theoretical foundation for Chinese medicine.

question as a whole rather than a part: "The way to verify: Check with strict criterion and Evaluate with synthetic analysis," and "To judge an opinion, one must put it into geographic and climatic context, and test it practically and using reasonable thinking. It proves true when it accords with the four factors," (*The Eight Ways to Rule*). It is obvious that Han Fei and Sun Tzu took similar views. They both thought that whether an idea was true or not depended on many factors, including geographic conditions, climatic conditions, its practical application, and reasonable thinking. Only once these four factors had been considered would a problem be resolved truthfully.

The idea of Synthesis was widely used in ancient Chinese medicine. In *The Inner Canon of the Yellow Emperor*, it was recorded that:

**A skillful doctor cures via synthesizing the symptoms. (*Basic Questions – The Influence of Geography, Climate, and Living Habit on Human*)**

**A doctor who synthesizes the symptoms and analyzes the disease can be called a master doctor. (*Central Area, On the Bad Blood in Zang and Fu*)**

According to *The Inner Canon of the Yellow Emperor*, a doctor who undertook a synthetic analysis of a disease would get rather different results than one who did not. The idea of Synthesis was embodied in the advice contained in *The Inner Canon of the Yellow Emperor* in three ways. Firstly, a doctor must obtain a comprehensive understanding of a disease by observing it fully: "A good doctor should observe the patient's complexion and take his pulse to decide *Yin* and *Yang* quality," (*Basic Questions, On Yin and Yang*). It was a rule in Chinese medicine that when a doctor diagnosed a disease using the *Four-Methods*, he must first decide on his patient's *Yin-Yang* quality (the four diagnostic methods in traditional Chinese medicine were: *Wang* (Observing), *Wen* (Smelling), *Wen* (Consulting), and *Qie* (Pulse-Taking)). Second, a doctor must observe his patient carefully and fully: "A doctor should also observe the patient's muscle, hard or soft; pulse, strong or weak, quick or slow; skin, cold or warm, dry or wet," ("Central Area, Evil *Qi*"). In accordance with *The Inner Canon of the Yellow Emperor*, the more carefully a doctor observed his patient, the more accurate his judgment would be. Thirdly, a doctor must consider more complicated factors: "A doctor should learn the laws in the Heaven and the Earth, as well as the human society," (*Basic Questions, On the Medical Truth*). In other words, the diagnosis of disease covered such factors as astronomy, geography, gender, age, power and wealth. Therefore, the idea of Synthesis or Synthetic Thinking in *The Inner Canon of the Yellow Emperor* was multi-faceted. It encompassed the syntheses of subjective methods, and assessed "all factors in one thing, and all factors out of one thing". In a word, the idea of Synthesis was completely embodied in *The Inner Canon of the Yellow Emperor*. In fact, the idea of Synthesis represented the central values of ancient Chinese medicine, which have been recognized (and which are reflected) in modern Chinese medicine.

## Association

The final main aspect of the holistic outlook was the idea which, today, we call Association. According to the idea of Association, a single phenomenon or objects do not exist in isolation, rather they are related to other phenomena or objects. In other words, all things exist as part of a whole or structure. As a result, people should consider things to be associated rather than isolated. One example of this idea can be found in ancient Chinese medicine.

According to *The Inner Canon of the Yellow Emperor*, a person's body was composed of five organs in Zang and six organs in Fu that were inter-connected. In *Basic Questions*, *Six Zang* and *Six Fu in Human Body*, there is the following famous passage:

**Yellow Emperor said, "I want to know the duty and status of the 12 organs in the human body."**

**Qi Bo answered, "So specific is your question! Let me discuss one by one. The heart is like a king and controls the person's movement; the lungs are like a prime minister and coordinate movement; the liver is like a general and takes strategy; the gallbladder is like a judge and makes judgment; the *Shan Zhong* is like an envoy and expresses joy or anger; the spleen and stomach are like officials in charge of food supply and affect nutrition; the large intestine is like a carrier and transports waste matter; the small intestine is like a container and discharges waste matter; the kidney is like a supporter and provides power to the person; the Three Burners (*San Jiao*) is like an official in charge of watercourses and controls the channel for discharge; the bladder is like a prefecture-level official and collects and discharges urine. Although they function dependently, they are not separate."**

As the above suggests, the human body was thought of as being like a governmental organization, in which the offices work independently but cannot exist alone as they fulfill their duties by coordinating with each other.

*The Inner Canon of the Yellow Emperor* expounded on the idea of Association in detail. First, it asserted that the five organs in *Zang* and the six organs in *Fu* were interconnected. In *Zang*, their relationship was "Heart rules kidney, lungs rule heart, liver rules lungs, spleen rules liver, kidney rules spleen," (*Basic Questions, The Formation of the Five Organs*). For *Zang* and *Fu*, their relationship was "Lung relates to large intestine, heart relates to small intestine, liver relates to gallbladder, spleen relates to stomach, kidney relates to bladder," (*Central Area, Acupuncture Point*). Second, it asserted that the relationship between *Zang* and *Fu* caused the interaction of diseases and the transfer of diseases between the organs in *Zang*: "When the kidney moves cold to the spleen, carbuncles and shortness of breath occur, when the spleen moves cold to the liver, carbuncles and spasms occur, when the liver moves cold to the heart, diseases intensify and choking occurs," (*Basic Questions, On Cold and Warm Qi in Human Body*). The way in which diseases were transferred between organs in *Zang* and *Fu* was described as follows: "When a cough is at the spleen, the stomach suffers, when it is at the liver, the gallbladder suffers, when it is at the lungs, the large intestine suffers," (*On Cough*). In addition, *The Inner Canon of the Yellow Emperor* suggested that there was not only interaction between *Zang* and *Fu*, but also between *Zang-Fu* and a person's body. This interaction was presented in three ways. The first was in relation to appearance: "When heart harmonizes with pulse, it benefits blood," and "When lung harmonizes with skin, it benefits skin," (*The Formation of the Five Organs*). The second was in relation to bodily associations: "The liver relates to the eyes, the spleen to the mouth, the kidney to *Er Yin* (the pubic region)," (*Discussion on the Important Ideas in the Golden Chamber*). The third was in relation to acupuncture points. According to Chinese Meridian Theory, the organs in *Zang* were connected with the body via the meridian system, which formed many acupuncture points. To conclude, it was thought that disease could be understood through the interaction of *Zang-Fu* and body and that diseases could be cured

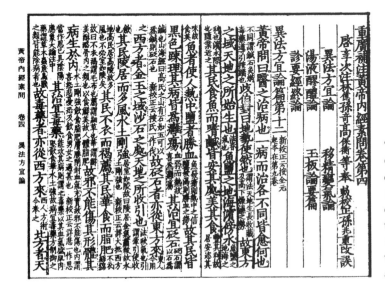

"Basic Questions: The Influence of Geography, Climate, and Living Habit on Human" in *The Inner Canon of the Yellow Emperor* (Part). "Basic Questions" consisted of 81 articles and covered theories on subjects such as heath care, *Yin-Yang*, the Five Elements, viscera and their symptoms, pathogenesis, diagnosis and treatment.

through the interaction of acupuncture points and *Zang*.

It should be noted that the association of the five organs in *The Inner Canon of the Yellow Emperor* was based on the Five Elements Theory that was popular in ancient China. However, the Five Elements Theory was not put into universal use in medicine, as it could not simply explain the associations of the human body. However, regardless of how it was specifically used, the idea of Association in *The Inner Canon of the Yellow Emperor* was certainly valuable, as has been confirmed by modern medicine.

孔子入周問禮樂至此

# WHAT ARE SOCIAL NORMS?

What are social norms or what should the ideal society be like? These were important issues to the ancient Chinese. As early as the Zhou Dynasty, the idea of Morality was seen in terms of "dedicating life and protecting people." Later, upholding morality became a basic tradition of the Chinese people. In the Confucian view, social norms could be summarized as Rite (*Li*), Benevolence (*Ren*), Righteousness (*Yi*) and Reason (*Li*). Indeed, Rite (*Li*) and Benevolence (*Ren*) have been important ideas for Chinese philosophy since the time of Confucius.

Mencius and Xun Zi interpeted Confucius's thought in different ways and proposed "benevolent rule" and "propriety and law" respectively. In addition, Confucians used an assessment of "righteousness vs. profit" and "heavenly principle vs. human desire" to judge right and wrong. Taoists and Legalists in Pre-Qin times also stated their views and theories on social issues, but these were quite different the thoughts of Confucians. Taoists held a negative attitude towards civilization and took a passive and retrogressive stance, but their criticism had a profound value. Legalists pursued the new and reformed the old. They were more objective and practical. Their views on the law, in particular, marked a great step forward for equality and justice in society. Of course, their discourse on political trickery seemed insidious and immoral. Their views on history played an important part in ancient Chinese philosophy.

# Moral Consciousness and the Establishment of Confucian Moral Principles

In China, social norms were originally established based on the idea of moral consciousness. This differentiated China from civilizations that relied a set of beliefs to shape the way in which people were expected to behave. Thanks to the efforts of Confucius, Rite (*Li*) and Benevolence (*Ren*) became two of the core ideas that the Chinese used to guide their behavior. As a result, Confucian moral principles became established.

## The Zhou Dynasty: the Origin of the Sense of Morality

The Chinese people's sense of morality started with the idea Filial Piety, which related to the clan system and to ancestral worship. In the Shang and Zhou dynasties (especially during the latter), the clan system was complete and people identified strongly with their clans. Therefore the idea of Filial Piety became an important moral idea.

The idea of Filial Piety was based on the parent-son relationship. The *Book of Documents* set up a model for filial piety: "When a man is not busy with farming, he should take goods with an oxcart and go far to trade. After he comes back, he should support his parents and show his filial piety. Only when his parents live happily can he drink," (*Edict of Prohibiting Drinking*). This meant that a man should work for his parent. It also meant that a man should only enjoy comfort after his parents had, and that he must worry before his parents worry and enjoy pleasure only after his parents have enjoyed it. Then the idea of Filial Piety was extended to cover the worship of ancestors and the respect that was due to brothers (the idea of *Ti*):

> Duke of Zhou hails it as a great accomplishment so that the descendants can popularize their ancestor's achievements and follow the Heaven's order. (*Book of Documents, Memorial Written in Luo State*)
>
> We should respect each other like brothers and make morality long. (*Classic of Poetry, Minor Court Hymns, High Wormwood*)

In the *Book of Documents*, the idea was discussed in a more humane way. This approach shared some similarities with the views of Mencius and Zhang Zai: "You must not dis-esteem the old or adults, nor the parentless or young," (*Pan Geng I*). In addition, the idea of Filial Piety became a virtue and a source of happiness, as well as a rule that applied to both rulers and citizens:

> One must always bear filial piety in mind and takes it as the rule in life. (*Classic of Poetry, Major Court Hymns, Successor to the Three Dynasties*)

*Portrait of Duke of Zhou,* displayed in the in Hall of South Fragrance in the Palace Museum. Duke of Zhou (1079-974 BC), also known as Ji Dan, was the son of King Wen of the Zhou Dynasty. When the King of Wu died, King Cheng ascended the throne. As King Cheng was young, the Duke of Zhou ruled as a regent. To consolidate the rule of Zhou Dynasty, the Duke of Zhou established systems for rite and music. He was one of the sages who were worshipped by later Confucians.

Stele with inscriptions of "Confucius Asking Rite and Music in Luoyang" in Luoyang. It was said that Confucius once came to Luoyang (also called Zhou, capital of Eastern Zhou Dynasty) and asked Lao Tzu rite and music. The stele was built in 1727, the 5th year of Emperor Yongzheng of Qing Dynasty.

**A man who is filial forever can be blessed forever. (*Classic of Poetry, Major Court Hymns, Drinking after Sacrifice*)**

"Being filial forever, being blessed forever" - this has been the way in which Filial Piety has been thought about in China for more than 3,000 years[20].

In the Zhou Dynasty, however, people viewed the ideas of Filial Piety and Morality differently: "You are assisted by many talents; you are filial and virtuous. You should lead them to assist you. You are respectable king. You are the model of citizens," (*Classic of Poetry, Major Court Hymns, Sinuous Mountain*). Some scholars also noted that "People in the Zhou Dynasty equally value the ideas of Filial Piety and Morality. The former to the Heaven and the latter to ancestors." [21]

The idea of Morality can be traced back as far as the Shang Dynasty: "No matter [if they are] distant or close relatives of the king, they must be punished with death when they commit crimes and rewarded with morality when they make contributions," (*Book of Documents, Pan Geng I*). The idea of Morality, however, developed in the Zhou Dynasty, specifically when the Duke of Zhou assisted the ruler. When compared with other world civilizations, it is therefore clear that the Chinese boasted the earliest understanding of the idea of Morality. In the *Book of Documents*, there were many records about this subject:

---

20. In Judaism, there is also the idea of Filial Piety, for instance, the Fifth of *The Ten Commandments*.

21. Hou Wailu, *A General History of Chinese Thought*. Beijing: People's Publishing House, 1957, p. 92.

King of Wen, your great and wise father, values morality and uses punishment with caution. He never dis-esteems the widowed. (*Appointment of Kang Shu*)

That is to say, you can behave in accordance with morality if you often examine yoursellf. (*Edict of Prohibiting Drinking*)

We may ask, why did the Duke of Zhou value the idea of Morality so much? What did his thoughts on the idea of Morality comprise? Which kind of model did it put forward and how did it impact on the future?

As suggested above, people in the Shang Dynasty stressed the importance of the Heaven's order and the Divine-right Theory of Kingship, which was common among many ancient civilizations. One of the Duke of Zhou's most important contributions was that he proposed the idea of Kingship based on the concept of Respect for Morality. This meant that a king should first respect morality in order to obtain the divine right to rule: "When the king does not know and respect morality, he is no longer credible to the Heaven and cannot maintain the Heaven's order long," (*Duke Zhao*). Moreover, the Duke of Zhou drew lessons from the experiences of the Xia and Shang dynasties:

We must draw lessons from Xia and Shang dynasties. They lost the Heaven's order soon… because they did not pay attention to their morality. Now that your majesty has been given the Heaven's order to rule the country, we must explore why they rose and fell so that you can maintain the Heaven's order… Your majesty should cultivate morality soon. I hope your majesty will carry out a benevolent rule to ensure that the Heaven's order will be sustained. (*Duke Zhao's Memorial to the King*)

The lessons that the Duke of Zhou leant from the Xia and Shang dynasties were that the king would obtain the Heaven's order if he adhered to morality and that he would lose the Heaven's order if he gave up morality. For this reason, the Duke of Zhao recommended that, when the King of Cheng ascended the throne, he should learn from the past, respect morality and so maintain the

Heaven's order. Meanwhile, Duke of Zhou proposed the idea "respecting morality and protecting people":

> Only when people live and work happily will the country be prosperous and peaceful: "I hope people will live in happiness and enjoy good health. We must remember the great virtue of the ancestors and take people's living and working happily as our pursuit." (*Appointment of Kang Shu*)

> The Heaven shows mercy to people, and the ruler should respect morality: "The Heaven expresses sympathy to people and transfers the order to us, so we must respect morality." (*Duke Zhao's Memorial to the King*)

> The ruler must take people as his mirror: "A ruler should take people rather than water as his mirror." (*Edict of Prohibiting Drinking*)

It can be seen that, by the time of the Zhou Dynasty, "respecting people" had become an essential part of the politics and philosophy of ancient China.

Meantime, Duke of Zhou concerned himself with the idea of benevolent rule. As is well known, Confucians (such as Confucius, Mencius and Xun Zi) discussed and advocated benevolent rule. The Duke of Zhou discussed in the issue in the *Appointment of Kang Shu*, in which he advised that a ruler should have a keen sense of morality and that he should often examine himself: "You should strive to benefit people, keep a calm mind and examine your thoughts and conduct." He also advised that a ruler would have deviated from benevolent rule if he disregarded people: "If you help the petty person to do evil and abandon your duty, you act against benevolent rule." In *Talented Person*, it was written that benevolent rule could harmonize the king and officials and win the support of people from afar: "If the late king can understand benevolent rule and pacify people from afar, they will come to celebrate. Then he will be respected by citizens." In *Vassals*, it was stated that, "I, king of Zhou, worship the Heaven and value morality, so I was given the Heaven's order." This remark emphasized the importance of valuing moral education and it became the basis of Confucian values relating to the cultivation of morality. It was also recorded, "From him

(Cheng Tang) to Zu Yi, no rulers did not understand morality and did not punish with caution, nor educate their people with morality." This remark dealt with the relationship between ruling with benevolence and ruling with law, as well as the idea of "understanding morality and punishing with caution."

The idea of a benevolent ruler encompassed the conduct of both ruler and citizens and the Duke of Zhou warned rulers about the danger of comfort and laziness:

**A man who lives in comfort indulges himself in pleasure, not knowing the hardship in sowing and reaping or the farmer's labor.**

**When you ascend the throne, you must not indulge yourself in pleasure, comfort, play, and hunting. (*No Comfort*)**

In particular, the Duke of Zhou warned against drinking excessively: "The ruler of the Shang Dynasty indulged in drinking and became ambitionless. As a result, all drank so much so that the Heaven smelled it and put the Shang Dynasty to end." To avoid this, he declared that people who drank excessively could be killed. (*Edict of Prohibiting Drinking*).

The idea of Morality played an important role in all of the above considerations. If someone thought about morality, then this indicated that they were conscious of right and wrong and indicated their capacity for reasoning. Over time, the idea of Morality became the basic principle of the social norms of ancient China. In the Spring and Autumn Period, the idea of Morality was used as a guideline for behaviour by politicians. For instance, Guan Zhong, the prime minister of the Qin Kingdom, proposed that a country should be ruled with Four Virtues: Rite (*Li*), Righteousness (*Yi*), Purity (*Lian*) and Shame (*Chi*). In Guan Zi's view, if one of these was lost, the country would be shaken; if two were lost, the country would be endangered, if three were lost, the country would be subverted and if four were lost, the country would be destroyed. He also believed that a shaken country could be consolidated, an endangered country saved and a subverted country restored. However, a country that had been destroyed could not be reinstated. He also said that a country

would perish if the Four Virtues were not carried out, (*Guan Zi, Ruling Citizens*). From this, it is clear that the idea of Morality was thought to play a pivotal role in how well a country was ruled. It was, in fact, thought of as the moral foundation for political honesty and social stability.

## Confucius: the Tradition of Rites and the Spirit of Benevolence

Confucian moral principles were established in the time of Confucius.

We know that, to Confucius, the "Three Dynasties" (the Xia, Shang, and Zhou dynasties) represented the most ideal form that society could take. In particular, he celebrated the fact that during the Zhou Dynasty, the systems for Rite (*Li*), Music (*Yue*), and Decree (*Dian Zhang*) were "compete" and "solemn". As Confucius extolled, "The ritual system in the Zhou Dynasty developed from the Xia and Shang dynasties and looked complete. I abide by it." (*The Analects, Ba Yi*). However, in the Spring and Autumn Period the system of Rite collapsed and the system of Music was ruined. Due to this collapse of traditional codes of behavior, Confucius lamented:

> If the country is ruled with *Tao*, the ruler decides the Rite, Music, and expedition; if without *Tao*, the vassals decide. (*Ji Shi*)
>
> If the country is ruled with *Tao*, vassals will not come into power and citizens will not discuss the political affairs. (*Ji Shi*)
>
> If the name is not correct, what one says is not reasonable. Then, he cannot handle affairs. Then, Rite and Music cannot be popularized. Then, the legal punishment cannot be made properly. Then, citizens will have no law to follow. (*Zi Lu*)

It should be noticed that Confucius did not keep pace with social developments and historical change. However, this did not mean that Confucius obstinately followed the beaten track all the time, rather, that he considered the system to be changeable: "The Shang Dynasty deleted and supplemented the Rite it inherited from the Xia Dynasty, which was known to us. The Zhou

Dynasty deleted and supplemented the Rite it inherited from the Shang Dynasty, which was also known to us. If the successor to Zhou Dynasty did the same, it would be still known to us even after 3,000 years," (*Wei Zheng*). At the same time, Confucius stressed that one could delete or supplement Rite, but that one must not overstep one's authority. For Confucius, the systems of Rite and Music were fundamentally hierarchical: "The ruler must act like a ruler; the official must act like an official; the father must act like a father; the son must act like a son," (*Yan Yuan*). Confucius thought that, if one transgressed this hierarchy, then Rite and Music would only be a meaningless form: "When one says Rite, does he just refer to jade and silk? When one says Music, does he just refer to bell and drum?" (*Yang Huo*). Therefore, Confucius' educational thoughts were based on Rite:

**A man who is respectful but does not know Rite will worry; who is cautious but does not know**

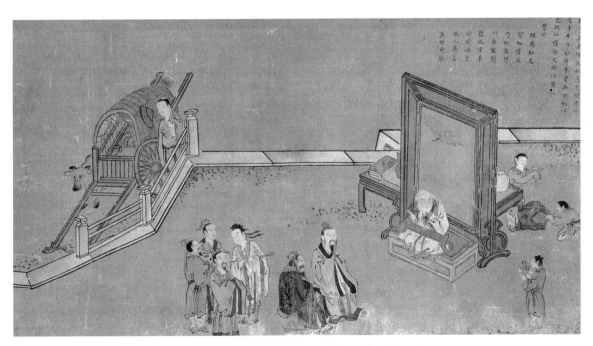

"Asking Lao Tzu Rite" from *Great Deeds of Confucius*, colored silk painting, Ming Dynasty.

Rite will seem timid; who is valorous but does not know Rite will make trouble; who is frank but does not know Rite will hurt others. (*Tai Bo*)

A man who does not learn Rite cannot act. (*Ji Shi*)

Confucians later inherited Confucius' thoughts on Rite. In fact, in ancient Chinese culture, the idea of Rite had multiple meaning. It could be understood as hierarchy and its associated set of etiquettes. Or it could be understood as politeness at the moral level. With respect to politeness, it was related to the idea of *Rang* (courteous action). It referred to both the courtesy between relatives (e.g. respecting the old and helping the young) and the courtesy between rivals (like retreating about thirty miles as a condition for peace).

Accordingly, Confucius mentioned the idea of Rite when he discussed the idea of Benevolence: "If a man lacks the quality of benevolence, how could he conform to Rite and Music?" (*Ba Yi*). "Benevolence means that one must return to Rite and restrain oneself. When all achieve this, benevolence will come out in the country," (*Yan Yuan*). When Yan Yuan asked how one should act with benevolence, Confucius replied, "One must not see, hear, speak, and do anything that disaccords with Rite." Although Confucius mentioned Rite again here, the ideas of Benevolence and Rite differed greatly. The idea of Benevolence was not a system (like Rite) but a morality, quality or spirit. As a matter of fact, the word Benevolence appeared in the Spring and Autumn Period. It was Confucius who endowed it with humane significance and turned it into the most essential and important idea in Confucianism.

Admittedly, Confucius' thoughts of the idea of Benevolence were based on those aspects of the ideas of Filial Piety and of Respect that related to kinship. You Ruo, a disciple of Confucius, said, "Filial piety toward a parent and respect for brothers are the cardinal rule for man." (*Xue Er*) Compared with the idea of Universal Love proposed by Mo Zi, Confucius' thoughts (which start from familial benevolence) seem limited. However, we must notice that Confucius' thoughts of the idea of Benevolence went further than that. To Confucius, the essence of the idea of Benevolence referred to more universal care or love:

**Students, when you are at home, be filial to your parents. When you are out, be respectful to your brothers. When you act, be careful and honest. You should show love to others and make acquaintance with the benevolent people. (*Xue Er*)**

**Fan Chi asked what benevolence was. Confucius replied, "Loving others." (*Yan Yuan*)**

Here, the idea of Benevolence included both loving family members and others. Confucius' universal care or love was also expressed in everyday ways. For example, in "Xiang Dang," it was recorded that when a horse stable caught fire, Confucius' first concern first was whether any person had been burnt. Confucius elucidated the essence of the universal care or love as follows:

**A man who is respectful, lenient, honest, intelligent, and kind can do benevolence to others. To be respectful will not bring him insult; to be lenient will win other's support; to be honest will obtain other's trust; to be intelligent will help him to make more**

Confucius (551-479 BC) was a great philosopher and educator in China. He founded Confucianism in the late Spring and Autumn Period. Politically, Confucius advocated a passive obedience to rite and stressed the importance of benevolence. From the Han Dynasty onwards, Confucius' theories became the orthodox way of thinking for the feudal Chinese.

Illustration in *Three Character Classic for Children Learning with Illustrations*: Confucius Composing the *Classic of Filial Piety*, drawn by Jinzhang Bookstore in the early Republic of China.

Illustration in *Three Character Classic for Children Learning with Illustrations*: Confucius Telling *Tao*, drawn by Jinzhang Bookstore in the early Republic of China.

contributions; to be kind will help him to order others. (*Yang Huo*)

Be considerate: One can practice benevolence when he puts himself in an other's position. (*Yong Ye*)

Be strict with oneself and tolerant to others: One should examine more himself and blame others less. (*King Ling of Wei*)

Subsequently, Confucius' idea of universal care or love became the fundamental principle by which Confucians and many other Chinese people treated others, handled their affairs and viewed things. The reason for this was summed up by Zhang Zai, who stated in *Correcting the Unenlightened*, "People, my compatriot; nature, my congener." In short, the idea of Benevolence ruled that one should treat others with tolerance and live with virtue. In this sense, it was the same as the idea of Charity found in Christianity and the idea of Mercy found in Buddhism.

# The Development of Confucian Social Norms

The systematic set of Confucian social norms were based on Confucius' thoughts on benevolence. Mencius and Xun Zi took up Confucius' thoughts in different ways and proposed "benevolent rule" and "propriety and law" respectively. An assessment of "righteousness vs. profit" and "heavenly principle vs. human desire" was used to judge right and wrong by Confucians in Pre-Qin time and during the Song and Ming dynasties. In addition, edification became thought of as the most important way to run the country and to give people peace.

## Mencius' Idea of Benevolent Rule and Xun Zi's Idea of "Propriety and Law"

Mencius' idea of benevolent rule developed from Confucius's thoughts on benevolence: "One should respect the old in his family as well as in others; one should love the young in his family as well as in others," (*Mencius, King Hui of Liang I*). Mencius set out a humane politics, which basically included domestic (ruling a country) and foreign affairs (diplomatic relations). Mencius believed that it was important to "protect a citizen's property," (*King Hui of Liang I*) and to "collect tax from citizens moderately," (*Duke of Wen of Teng I*). Mencius stated that, "In a yard with an area of five mu, one can plant mulberry so that people over 50 can wear bombazine clothes, and one can rear chicken, a dog, or a pig so that people over 70 can eat meat. In a farmland with an area of 100 *mu*, one can work hard so that several families can have food," (*King Hui of Liang I*). In this way, Mencius suggested that the ruler should ensure that the basic needs of each citizen are met (this idea was also known as "to protect citizen's property" or "inviolable property"). He also stated

that, "Those who possess property will have a sense of morality; those who lack property will have no sense of morality," (*Duke of Wen of Teng I*). In addition, Mencius claimed that a ruler "should abolish legal punishment and reduce tax," (*King Hui of Liang I*). This approach was also known as "to collect tax from citizens moderately." According to Mencius, a tyrannical ruler would make citizens obedient using power but a benevolent ruler would use morality. He noted: "With power, citizens obey against their will; with morality, citizens obey with sincerity," (*Gong Sun Chou I*).

Furthermore, Mencius proposed a view that fundamentally influenced the course of thinking in China. This was summed up in the phrase: "Citizens, valuable; Ruler, light." Mencius said, "A vassal has three treasures: land, citizen, and political talent," (*With All Heart II*). For him, citizens were the most valuable of these three treasures: "Citizens are the most important, the state the second, and the ruler the third," (*With All Heart II*). Mencius also denounced vassals who acted in ways that caused great calamity to citizens:

> **There is delicious meat in their kitchen and strong horses in their stable, but citizens suffer starvation and some die out. This differs nothing from eating people along with beasts. (*Duke of Wen of Teng II*)**

> **When vassals vied for a land, the killed covered the battlefield; when vassals vied for a city, the killed covered the city. This equals that one eats human's flesh. The crime is so heinous that to kill them seems too light. (*Li Lou I*)**

Mencius stated that if a ruler was tyrannical, then his citizens could subvert him. He said: "A ruler who disobeys benevolent rule is a thief; who disrespects is a villain; who does both is a tyrant. When Zhou was killed, no one viewed it as regicide," (*King Hui of Liang II*). In the West, similar thoughts were proposed by Locke and Rousseau in the 18th century. In China, however, it had been an important theory nearly 2,000 years earlier – one that witnessed many changes of dynasty.

Xun Zi advocated the equality of "propriety and law" or "the value of both propriety and law". He said: "One who values propriety and respects the talent can be a ruler; one who values law and

Illustration in *Three Character Classic for Children Learning with Illustrations*: Mencius Talking with King of Qi, drawn by Jinzhang Bookstore in the early Republic of China.

protects people can be an overlord," (*Xun Zi, Prosperity of the Country*). Obviously, Xun Zi's idea of Propriety developed from Confucius' thought and his idea of Law embodied Legalist thinking. This shows that Xun Zi partially recognized Legalism and that he had a deep understanding of social management. To Xun Zi, a complete system of social management should consist of propriety and law: "Only when propriety is valued and law is completed will a country enjoy good order," (*The Law for Ruling Country*). At the same time, Xun Zi emphasized that propriety should be the guiding principle of law. For example, he said: "Book of Rites is the general principle of laws and rules," (*Encouraging Learning*). In this statement, Xun Zi highlighted his Confucian stance. However, his idea of "propriety and law" broke the boundary between Confucianism and Legalism and integrated the thoughts of the two schools.

In some cases, Xun Zi's discourse did not distinctly differentiate propriety and law. For example, he said: "Propriety, the start of prosperity," (*System and Law for the Ruler*), and, "Law, the start of prosperity," (*The Law for Ruling Country*). Overall, he thought that it was propriety and law "as a whole" that was indispensable to the smooth running of a society and a country.

Xun Zi also proposed an important sociological thought, which he termed the "Division and Mutual Reliance between People". The importance of this is summed up in the following quotation: "People are weaker than cattle and slower than horses, but people can drive them. Why? People can

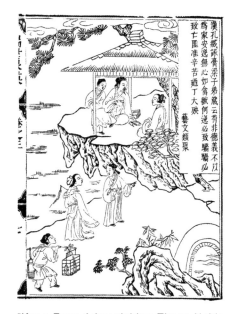

"Kong Zang Admonishing Those Noble Descendants," from *Collections of Literary Theory and Works*, Vol. 3, *Masterpieces in the Prosperous Time*, Ming Dynasty. Kong Zang was part of the 11<sup>th</sup> generation of Confucius' family. In the reign of Emperor Wen during the Western Han Dynasty, he inherited the title of Marquis of Liao, won the honor of *Bo Shi* (erudite scholar) was appointed *Tai Chang* (Minister of Ceremonies) and became one of the Nine Ministers in the court. He warned the "noble descendents" that there would be no harmony in a country if it was not ruled with rite, that there would be no difference between animals and humankind if people indulged in comfort and lost ambition, and that citizens would suffer if a ruler considered ruling a country hard.

form communities but cattle and horses cannot," (*System and Law for the Ruler*). Here Xun Zi was referring to the natural and social attributes of human societies. He also discussed why people form communities and highlighted the issue of "Division". He said: "People cannot live without a community, but they will be rivals without division," (*System and Law for the Ruler*). By "division," Xun Zi meant social differentiations based on duty, grade, and class: "It is difficult for a man to possess many skills and to undertake several posts. If people live solitarily, they will lose help; if people live socially, they will be rivals. To lose help is a trouble; to be rivals is a disaster. The best way to avoid both is to differentiate people and make them live in a community," (*Enriching the Country*). For Xun Zi, it was most important to differentiate people equally: "Therefore, the late king established propriety and differentiated the citizens, noble or humble, old or young, intelligent or stupid, talented or talentless. Based on their abilities, citizens undertook different jobs and obtained different payments. Ultimately, they lived in a community and existed in harmony," (*Shame and Honor*). Xun Zi also proved the idea of Division ontologically: "There will be no difference if things are divided averagely; there will be no authority if power is divided averagely; there will be no inferiority if payment is divided averagely … Two noble men cannot serve each other, neither can two humble men. That is the natural law," (*System and Law for the Ruler*). In some sense, Xun Zi's thought on "Division and Mutual Reliance between People" established a solid sociological foundation for a political theory based on the idea of "the value of both propriety and law." From today's perspective, it is clear that he was concerned about conflict and balance between individuals and between individuals and society. In this sense, his thoughts still have real value.

## Edification and the Ethical Tradition of Chinese Civilization

With respect to social norms, the philosophers of ancient China had a long tradition of valuing education, cultivation or edification. This started with the education of aristocrats in the Zhou Dynasty. From long experience, ancient Chinese philosophers came to realize that a man would not behave decently if he had not received an education. In addition, they realized that human nature could have weaknesses, and that these could only be restrained or corrected through education or edification. Therefore, they thought that it was not enough for a ruler to only think about his people's livelihoods, he should also think about their education. Amongst Confucians, it was widely known that Confucius was an educator. Mencius also stressed that citizens must be edified when they became rich. He made the following comment on education: "The ruler should endeavor to establish schools and to educate people with the ideas of Filial Piety and Respect. Then, the old who carries things on the road would be

"Xu Jing Educating Citizens Rite and Law," from *Collected Anecdotes in Chinese History*, Vol. 2, *Masterpieces in the Prosperous Time*. It was recorded that in the Eastern Han Dynasty, Xu Jing was promoted to be the prefect of Guiyang, where citizens acted unruly and knew little rite. Xu Jing made rules for funerals and weddings and publicized rite and laws amongst them. He was highly praised by citizens during his 12-year-career, and they built a temple and stele for him.

"Moral and Ethical Values Series". A stamp issued by Macao Post, in November 2007. Taking moral and ethical values as its theme, the series featured four Chinese characters *Dao* (Tao), *De* (Morality), *Lun* (Ethic), and *Li* (Rite), and the images of four Chinese sages Lao Tzu, Chuang Tzu, Confucius and Mencius on stamps. This was done to display the development of Chinese morality and ethics.

helped by the young," (*Mencius, King Hui of Liang II*). Mencius attached more importance to good education than to good rule: "With good rule, citizens fear the ruler; with good education, citizens respect the ruler. Good rule brings the ruler the citizens' wealth; good education brings him the citizens' hearts," (*With All Heart I*). Xun Zi's view on edification was based on his theory Hua Xing Qi Wei (to guide and reform human nature with propriety and law). He said: "We cannot change a man's nature but we can reform it. We cannot achieve anything when we are born, but we can achieve things with effort," (*Xun Zi, The Role of Confucian*). He also stressed, "The ruler should edify citizens with propriety and law so that they understand the need to be respectful and modest. Then, the citizens will behave well and the country will enjoy peace," (*The Evil of Human Nature*).

The sense of shame was an important part of edification. As mentioned above, in the Spring and Autumn Period, Guan Zi listed it as one of the four principles for ruling a country. Later, Confucianism viewed the sense of shame as an essential and cardinal social norm, and it was fully represented in the thoughts of Confucius and Mencius. In *The Analects*, the sense of shame was mentioned 17 times. For instance:

A man will not humiliate himself if he acts in accordance with rite. (*Xue Er*)

If a ruler edifies citizens with morality and governs citizens with rite, they will know shame and law. (*Wei Zheng*)

Confucius said, "A man flatters with sweet words and ingratiating smile. Zuo Qingming views that as a shame, so do I." (*Gong Ye Chang*)

A man should not do what he views shameful. (*Zi Lu*)

A gentleman views it as a shame when one brags but never acts. (*Xian Wen*)

In Mencius, the sense of shame was mentioned 19 times. For instance,

A gentleman views it as a shame when one's fame disaccords with his action. (*Li Lou II*)

Human must not lack the sense of shame. When one takes the lack of the sense of shame as a shame, he will not be shamed. (*With All Heart I*)

The sense of shame does matter! One who plays tricks does not feel shameful. (*With All Heart I*)

The sense of shame was also mentioned in the *Book of Rites*: "One who knows shame will have the courage to correct," (*Golden Mean*). The sense of shame also related to the idea of Purity, as was stated in Guan Zi, "Citizens should know shame and officials know purity." In the late Ming and early Qing Dynasty, Gu Yanwu expounded on this theme in the following way: "Therefore, a corrupt man acts against rite and righteousness because he lacks the sense of shame. It is a shame for a country when the officials do not understand shame," (*Notes Taken in Daily Reading,* Vol. 13 *Honor and Shame*). It can be clearly seen that the cultivation of a person's sense of shame was an important part of the Confucian idea of Edification, which in turn, laid the moral foundation for ruling the country.

Feng Youlan in the 1950s. Feng Youlan (1895-1990), was a renowned contemporary Chinese philosopher. He was born in Tanghe, Henan Province. In 1924, he obtained a PhD degree from Columbia University. He was a Professor at Zhongzhou University (today Henan University), Guangdong University and Yanching University. He was also Dean of the School of Liberal Arts and Chair of the Department of Philosophy at Tsinghua University, Professor at the Department of Philosophy and Dean of the School of Liberal Arts at the National Southwestern Associated University, Chairman of the University Council at Tsinghua University and a Professor of the Department of Philosophy at Peking University. His philosophical works played a vital role in the establishment of philosophy as a discipline in China.

The idea of Edification was particularly valued during the Song Dynasty. Thanks to the efforts of Confucians, the clan system of common citizens was formed during this time. The clan system then became the focus for the development of clan instruction, clan rule, clan property, pedigree and familial knowledge. In addition, many *Shu Yuan* were established. These were places where children or scholars read Confucian classics. They facilitated the dissemination of Confucianism from aristocrats to citizens. In addition, *Zhu Xi* systematically studied the education of children and formed the rules for *Xiao Xue* education, which corresponded to or supplemented *Da Xue* education. [Note: In ancient China, the education system consisted of *Xiao Xue* and *Da Xue*, both of which differed fundamentally from modern Chinese schools and universities. The former taught *Xun Gu* (the explanation of Chinese words) and the latter taught Confucian classics.] According to *Zhu Xi*, the things taught in *Xiao Xue* education was superficial and concerned "basic rite", and the things taught in *Da Xue* education were profound and concerned state affairs. (These thoughts were recorded in *Keys Remarks on Xiao Xue Education*). Some of the books written by Zhu Xi, such as *Xiao Xue Education and Knowledge Children Must Know*, played an important role in cultivating the morality of children in ancient China, as Feng Youlan acknowledged:

**Feng Youlan and *A Short History of Chinese Philosophy***

Feng Youlan devoted his whole life to reviving Chinese traditional culture and to publicizing Confucian philosophy. In 1947, he was lecturing at the University of Pennsylvania, teaching the history of Chinese philosophy. Based on this work, he wrote *A Short History of Chinese Philosophy*, which was published by Macmillan USA in 1948.

In its 200,000 words, *A Short History of Chinese Philosophy* narrates the history of Chinese philosophy and covers the knowledge of ancient and modern times and of China and the West. Concise as it might seem, it embodies Feng Youlan's understanding of Chinese philosophy and combines historical facts and insightful ideas. It is full of the wisdom of life and the insight of philosophers. It has been translated into many languages and has been used as the general textbook for Chinese philosophy courses in many universities and as an introductory book for people learning about Chinese culture. In China, it was translated into Chinese in the 1980s by one of Feng Youlan's students. In 1985, the Chinese edition was published by Peking University Press and became a bestselling academic book.

In China, philosophy is closely related to one's education. In ancient China, when a boy was educated, he was enlightened with philosophical thoughts. When he entered school, he was firstly taught *Four Books*, namely *The Analects, Mencius, Great Learning and Doctrine of the Mean*. These *Four books* had been the most important textbooks for New-Confucianist philosophy since the Song Dynasty. Rudimentary reading for children was often the *Three Character Classic* (*San Zi Jing*). With three characters in a group and six characters in a sentence, it was a textbook to learn characters and easy to read and remember. The first sentence was "When a person was born, his nature was good." This was actually the basic idea of Mencius's philosophy.[22]

Feng Youlan is referring here to the education that was embodied in the clan rule of the Song Dynasty. In *The Clan Instructions of the Zhang Family in Yanfu of Shangyu*, the instructions

---

22. Feng Youlan, *A Short History of Chinese Philosophy*, Chapter One "The Spirit of Chinese Philosophy."

included: be faithful to the ruler, filial to parents, respectful to brothers, differentiate husband from wife and be harmonious with relatives, educate descendants, inhere the deceased, improve skills, be diligent in work, economical in life, upright in character, prudent in words and behavior, modest in behavior and cautious in marriage, value funerals and sacrifice, construct ancestral temples, buy burial land, build tombstones, buy land for sacrifice, protect trees, do not steal, be strict in names, don't quarrel over lawsuits and do not use violence. In *The Clan Instructions of Xin Qigong of the Gao Family in Pangu*, the instructions included: be respectful to morality, cultivate morality, pay grain taxes quickly, value sacrificial ceremonies, choose the outstanding as leader, be strict in clan rule and in names, be diligent at learning morality, repair your house frequently, adhere to frugality, do not use obscenity, do not steal, do no quarrel over lawsuits, do not practice sorcery, do not lie or gamble, be respectful to knowledgeable men, courteous to the old and helpful to the poor, be cautious in making friends and cherish friendship. In *The Clan Instructions and Rules of the Long Family in Shouzhou*, there were 12 instructions and rules to reward good. These were: be respectful to ancestors, be filial to parents, revere teachers and seniors, be friendly to brothers, be clean in a woman's bedroom, be cautious in making friends, be harmonious with relatives, be diligent in study, value chastity and filial piety, be diligent in work and do good deeds to the deceased. There were also 12 instructions and rules to punish evil. These were: no defiance, no violence, no gambling, no excessive drinking, no theft, no forcible burial, no cutting trees, no obscenity, no refusing to pay taxes, no quarreling over lawsuits, no frivolity and no asperity.[23] In short, Confucianism ethics was deeply accepted by Chinese in a variety of subtle ways, and Confucianism expressed its best values through edification rather than through religion.

However, we must not disregard the negative values of Confucian ethnics, for example, the idea of the Three Cardinal Guides. This idea was actually formed before Confucianism, and was then consolidated once Confucianism had been formed. It is the very traditional view that the ruler should guide the subject, that the father should guide the son, and that the husband should

---

23. In fact, the clan rule was very similar to the commandments in Judaism. See Wu Chun, *The Ethical Life in Chinese Society: A Study of the Possibility of Confucianism in Ethics.* Beijing: Zhonghua Book Company, 2007.

guide the wife (as found in the *Views on Five Classics Collected in White Tiger Conference* from the Han Dynasty). The idea of the Three Cardinal Guides presented a merciless and dark set of commandments, especially when compared with the positive moralities and values that Confucianism also espoused. Over time, the irrational nature of this idea became more obvious, however this did not stop the idea from hindering social development.

## The Confucian View on "Righteousness vs. Profit" and "Heavenly Principle vs. Human Desire"

The social norm relating to "righteousness vs. profit" was formed as early as the Spring and Autumn Period and was subsequently greatly valued by Confucianism. To Confucians, the idea of Righteousness stood for justice or morality, while the idea of Profit stood for self-interest. *In The Analects*, Confucius said, "A gentleman takes righteousness as the fundamental principle (*Zhi*)," (*King Ling of Wei*). Here, Zhi meant source as in "Source-End" or noumenon as in "Noumenon-Function." Confucius also highlighted the uniqueness of righteousness:

> For a gentleman, there is no criterion to judge what is right or wrong but righteousness. (*Li Ren*)

He also highlighted the harm that the pursuit of profit could bring: "If a man acts just in accordance with his profit, others will bear him malice," (*Li Ren*). Here, Confucius made a choice between righteousness and profit. This was later acknowledged by his followers. For instance,

> It is enough for Your Majesty to know what righteousness and benevolence rather than profit mean. (*Mencius, King Hui of Liang I*)

> When righteousness prevails, the country will enjoy peace; when profit prevails, the country will undergo disturbance. (*Xun Zi, Strategies*)

Brick inscription of 100 styles of the Chinese character *Shou* (Longevity) on the screen wall of the door opposite the Qiao's Family Courtyard, Qixian County, Shanxi Province. Down the two sides runs a couplet in seal script written by Zuo Zongtang, a famous official from the Qing Dynasty. With great significance, the couplet reads: "One should restrain his desire to revive the heavenly principle; one should cultivate morality to write well." On the top are two Chinese characters *Lü He* (which mean Practicing Harmony), these accorded with the idea of "valuing harmony" that the Qiao family, a prestigious merchant family, followed.

**One makes acquaintance with others not to obtain profit; one helps other to publicize righteousness. (*The History of Han Dynasty, Biography of Dong Zhongshu*)**

In addition, the Confucian view on "righteousness vs. profit" differentiated the gentleman and the petty man:

**The gentleman concerns whether it accords with righteousness; the petty man concerns whether it brings him profit. (*The Analects, Li Ren*)**

**A man who strives for righteousness is a sage like Shun; a man who strives for profit is a theft like Zhi. (*Mencius, With All Heart I*)**

**People are born with bad nature. If they are not taught by teachers or restrained by law, they will pursue profit only. (*Xun Zi, Honor and Shame*)**

Wang Fuzhi, a philosopher who lived during the Ming Dynasty, also stressed that: "What differentiates a gentleman and a petty man, a human and an animal, is their view on righteousness and profit," (*My Reading of History as a Mirror, Wei Zi*). It is commendable that Confucians took righteousness or morality as the cardinal principle when they considered the righteousness-profit relationship. However, we should also notice their views were biased[24]. It should also be noted that some Confucian scholars had different opinions. In the Southern Song Dynasty, Chen Liang and Ye Shi put more emphasis on achievement and utility. In the late Ming Dynasty and the early Qing Dynasty, Yan Yuan changed Dong Zhongshu's sentences to "One should obtain profit while making acquaintances with others; one should consider his interest while publicizing righteousness," *(Correcting The Four Books*, vol. 1). In fact, it should be noted that Confucianism had a utilitarian

---

24. A similar view can be seen in Hegelianism: "Profit cannot exist as a special will but as a universal one. In essence, a thing is meaningful and dependent only when it exists as a universal and free one. Without law, profit cannot breed goodness." Hegel, *Grundlinien Der Philosophie Des Rechts*. Beijing: Commercial Press, 1982, p. 132.

nature from its very beginning, as shown by the value placed on accomplishments in the *Book of Documents and Profit in the Commentaries on Book of Change*.

The issue of "heavenly principle vs. human desire" was mentioned in such early Confucian classics as the *Record on the Subject of Music*: "People are born to be unselfish. That's the heavenly principle. They desire something when they see it. That's human desire… The heavenly principle will perish when people do not control and examine themselves but indulge in desire. There is no limit to the lure of things, nor to human desire. If human desire can be gratified with the endless pursuit of things, there will be no difference between people and things." The issue was widely discussed during the Song Dynasty. Theoretically, the issue of "heavenly principle vs. human desire" developed from the issue of "righteousness vs. profit." Principle, or the heavenly principle, can be understood as Righteousness. Desire, or human desire, can be understood as Profit. Obviously, this issue embodies the ideas of Neo-Confucianism and the Cheng-Zhu School of thought:

> **That human nature is incomprehensible refers to human desire; that human goodness is profound refers to heavenly principle. (Cheng Hao, *Posthumous Work of Mr. Cheng*, Vol. 11)**

> **What the sages say can be summarized as "teaching people the heavenly principle and eliminating the human desire." (Zhu Xi, *Words of Zhu Zi*, Vol. 12)**

> **What a man should learn is how to eliminate human desire and revive the heavenly principle. (Zhu Xi, *Words of Zhu Zi*, Vol. 13)**

It should be noted that the Cheng-Zhu School's views on "heavenly principle vs. human desire" were grounded on their reflections on moral and social issues. However, the School was mistaken in their belief that the heavenly principle was completely opposed to human desire. Followers of this school of thought therefore drew conclusions that were anti-humanistic or anti-nature. For instance:

When a man asked, "Could a widow who is lonely, poor, and helpless marry again?"

Cheng Yi replied, "People say this as they fear she will die of cold and hunger. To die of hunger is less important than to lose her virtue." (Cheng Yi, *Posthumous Work of Mr. Cheng*, Vol. 22)

Evidently, the idea of "Reviving the Heavenly Principle and Eliminating Human Desire" could bring disaster, as Dai Zhen, a scholar in the Qing Dynasty, observed:

With truth, the superior blames the inferior, the old blames the young, and the noble blames the humble. The former must be respected in spite that they are wrong. With truth, the inferior refutes the superior, the young refutes the old, and the humble refutes the noble. The former must not defy in spite of the fact that they are right. As a result, the lower can never be equal with the upper in human nature (emotion and desire). It is uncountable that it is the lower's fault although the upper's blame is wrong. People sympathize with those who are killed by law, but who cares about those who are killed by principle? (*Annotation of Mencius, Reason*)

In modern China, Cheng-Zhu School's views on "heavenly principle vs. human desire" have been criticized by many scholars. For instance, Lu Xun once said that he discovered two words in the 24 histories of China. These were "Eating Human".

# Reflections on Social Issues in Other Schools of Thought

In addition to Confucianism, there are some other Chinese schools of thought that deserve our attention. In Pre-Qin times, Taoism (represented by the philosophers Lao Tzu and Chuang Tzu), held opposite views to Confucianism (views that were encapsulated in the idea of non-action). Taoists also re-evaluated and criticized civilization in a profound way. Legalism appeared later than Confucianism. Legalism attached less importance to tradition and proposed a series of more constructive theories. However, the mercilessness and darkness of Legalism enormously undermined its positive values. It is notable that some Legalist thoughts were complementary to those of mainstream Confucianism and that some were directly absorbed by Confucianism.

## The Taoist Idea of Non-action

In contrast to Confucians, who extolled civilization, Taoists kept civilization "at an arm's length". Both Lao Tzu and Chuang Tzu harshly criticized civilization.

Lao Tzu stated,

> **Benevolence appears after Tao perishes; deceit appears after wisdom arises; filial piety forms after family harmony loses; faithful officials emerge when a country suffers disturbance. (*Lao Tzu*, Chapter 18)**

> **A man with great virtue does not present it; a man without virtue strives to present it. A man**

with great virtue follows the law and believes in non-action; a man without virtue pursues the form and does not act. A man with great benevolence displays it unconsciously; a man with great righteousness displays it consciously. A man with great rite will ask for when his action has not been rewarded. Therefore, virtue appears after Tao perishes; benevolence appears after virtue disappears; righteousness arises after benevolence has been lost; rite emerges after righteousness vanishes. Rite indicates the lack of faith and the start of disaster. (Chapter 38)

When there are more rulers in a country, citizens become more impoverished; when there are more weapons owned by citizens, a country suffers more wars; when there are more tricks, more treasures appear; when a ruler takes more from citizens using the law, thefts increase. (Chapter 57)

As mentioned above, Lao Tzu was dissatisfied with ideas such as wisdom, virtue, benevolence, righteousness, rite, filial piety, faithful officials, weapons, tricks, treasures and rules. In his view, these were the result of the abolition or loss of *Tao*.

Accordingly, Lao Tzu advocated that a ruler should rule based on non-action and that he should abandon wisdom, virtue, benevolence, righteousness, rite, and desire:

Do not admire the talented so that citizens will not vie for fame and profit. Do not value treasures, so that citizens will not steal. Do not show desirable things so that citizens will not be disturbed. Therefore, a sage's principal for rule is to eliminate the citizen's prejudice, to satisfy the citizen's appetite, to reduce the citizen's pursuit, to enhance the citizen's body, and to make citizens desireless, so that the talented cannot accomplish and the rule of non-action can be achieved. (Chapter 3)

If a ruler abolishes knowledge and wisdom, citizens can profit a hundredfold; if a ruler abolishes benevolence and righteousness, citizens become filial; if a ruler abolishes tricks and profit, theft disappears. (Chapter 19)

A ruler does nothing and citizens will cultivate themselves; a ruler remains calm and citizens will control themselves; a ruler makes no rules and citizens will become rich; a ruler has no desire and citizens will be simple. (Chapter 57)

*Five Old Taoists*, colored painting, in the corridor of the Summer Palace, Beijing. During the Northern Song Dynasty, the five famous officials Du Yan, Bi Shichang, Zhu Guan, Wang Huan, and Feng Ping often gathered and studied Taoism (they did this after they had resigned). They pursued a peaceful life of non-action, cultivated their minds, drunk with pleasure, and maintained good health. They died when they were over 80 years old and were subsequently known as the Five Old Taoists.

It is certain that Lao Tzu's views on the heavens extended to social issues. In addition, Lao Tzu severely criticized rulers who obtained things without toil and called them "leaders of theft" (*Dao Kua* in Chinese). He described them as follows: "they who live in grand palaces, abandon farming, empty the storehouse, wear elaborate adornment, carry sharp swords, pay too much attention to food, and accumulate wealth." (Chapter 53) Meanwhile, Lao Tzu set out a rather obscurantist stance to ruling: "A ruler following Tao should fool citizens rather than enlighten them. Citizens are hard to control as they have knowledge. Therefore, a ruler who rules with wisdom is an enemy to a country and a ruler who rules without wisdom brings bliss to a country." (Chapter 65). Therefore, Lao Tzu admired what he called "a Small Utopian Society":

**There was a country with so small an area and population that the various tools were of no use. People valued their life and never went far from their homes. There was nowhere to go with a boat or carriage and no place for armor and weapons. People recorded things by tying knots.**

People were gratified with food, clothes, a place to live and custom. Although they could see citizens in their neighborhood where roosters crowed and dogs barked, they never visited each other. (Chapter 80)

Chuang Tzu inherited the thoughts of Lao Tzu and opposed benevolence and virtue. Chuang Tzu said, "The worst is to pursue virtue with purpose, which meant to let the heart observe with the eyes," (*Chuang Tzu, Lie Yu Kou*). Here Chuang Tzu was suggesting that a man who pursued virtue on purpose was a hypocrite. Chuang Tzu also said that: "Love and interest come from benevolence. There are few who relinquish benevolence but more who take advantage of benevolence. To practice benevolence will breed dishonesty and become the tool of the wicked and avaricious man," (*Xu Wu Gui*). Like Lao Tzu, Chuang Tzu also despised wisdom and technology.

In "Heaven and Earth," the bifurcation of Confucianism and Taoism was expressed through the dialogue between Zi Gong and an old man:

Zi Gong travels in the Kingdom of Chu in the south. He sees an old man irrigating with a jar. Zi Gong says, "There is a machine that can irrigate 100 mu one day with less work and more efficiency. Why do you not try it?" The old man says, "How?" Zi Gong says, "The machine is made from wood. The back is heavy and the front is light. It pumps so quickly that the water looks like boiling. Its name is *Gao*. The old man becomes angry and flees, saying: "Machine results in tricks and tricks result in schemes. When there is a scheme in a man's heart, honesty is undermined; when honesty is undermined, spirit is disturbed, when spirit is disturbed, *Tao* cannot be carried. I refuse it not because I do not know it but because I feel shameful."

The old man rejected the machine because he thought that a man who used machines must play tricks and conduct schemes. Confucians worshiped *San Dai* (Xia, Shang, and Zhou dynasties) and followed Yao and Shun. However, Chuang Tzu denied them, saying: "The root of the riot lies in the reign of Yao and Shun, whose harm will appear 1,000 years later. Then, men will eat each other,"

(*Sang Geng Chu*). Chuang Tzu also took heavenly law as the principle by which people should govern their activities, saying: "It will harm nature to correct it with a try-square and a restrictive line. It will weaken virtue to consolidate it with rope and lacquer. It will deform citizens to reform, cultivate, and pacify them with rite, music and benevolence," (*Parallel Toe*). Here Chuang Tzu was comparing rite, music, and benevolence to the try-square and the restrictive line that constrained nature. So how did he think that human nature could remain normal? He said, "Do not act against heaven, do not destroy nature, and do not strive for fame." (*Qiu Shui*)

In particular, Chuang Tzu further developed Lao Tzu's idea of *Dao Kua* and revealed deep truths about the relationship between sages, aristocrats, and thiefs. He said, "Is there a man who is hailed as the most knowledgeable who does not steal like a thief? Is there a man who is hailed as the wisest who does not accumulate wealth like a thief?" Chuang Tzu replied to the view that even robbers had a code of conduct with Dao Zhi's words:

**A virtuous man can guess the treasure in a house, a brave man can vie for that treasure, a righteous man can withdraw, a wise man can predict the result, and a benevolent man can divide the treasure equally. There is no thief who possesses the five qualities.**

Chuang Tzu exposed inequity: "A man who steals a hook will be killed while a man who steals a country will be respected as a vassal." He stressed that: "There will be thefts when the sages live; there will be no thefts when the sages die," (*On Thievery*).

Biased as Chuang Tzu's views seemed, they were insightful. Generally, in the history of China and Chinese thought, Taoist views on social issues complemented the more orthodox views of Confucianism.

## The Legalist Idea of Rule by Law

Legalism was an important school of thought that concentrated on the idea of rule by law during the Warring States Period. The emergence of Legalism accorded with the challenges being faced at this time: How to treat tradition and face reality. Specifically, Legalism discussed how to balance the interests of the old and new classes, how to rule in a fair rather than a hereditary way, and how to maintain a leading position in a fiercely competitive race. In some sense, Legalism contradicted Confucianism which respected tradition and took a conservative attitude. Legalists included Li Kui, Wu Qi, Shang Yang, Shen Dao, Shen Buhai, Han Fei, and Li Si. Of these the key figures, Shang Yang and Han Fei, will be discussed.

The most important contribution made by Shang Yang was that he viewed history as dynamic process. He therefore said that a ruler must take appropriate measures:

> The law system in the past differs from that of the present, so there is no law to follow; the rites made by kings differ from each other, so there is no rite to follow. (*The Book of Lord Shang, Changing the Law*)

> The law and rite are made in accordance with time and need. (*The Book of Lord Shang, Changing the Law*)

> A sage does not follow the past, nor adhere to the present. A man who follows the past cannot keep pace with time; a man who adheres to the present cannot keep up with time. The Zhou Dynasty did not follow the Shang Dynasty, and the Xia Dynasty did not follow the Shun and Yu. All ruled the country in spite of the difference in rule. (*Opening and Debarring*)

Here Shang Yang was embodying the idea of pursuing the new and reforming the old, which is an objective and realistic approach. It was also the common feature of Legalist thought.

Han Fei inherited and developed the thoughts of Legalism. In particular, he elaborated on the content and the significance of law. He said, "The law should not favor the powerful people and the

"Shang Yang Being Turned Asunder by Carts," illustration in *Revised Chronicle of the States,* printed in the Ming Dynasty. Shang Yang (395-338 BC) was a politician, reformer, philosopher, and the representative of Legalism during the Warring States Period. With the support of the Duke of Xiao of the Qin Kingdom, Shang Yang reformed household registration, the ranking of the military and the nobility, land systems, administrative divisions, tax, metrology, and folk custom. He also made harsh laws. While they made the Qin Kingdom a power, Shang Yang's reforms impaired the interests of the nobility. After the Duke of Xiao died, Shang Yang was torn asunder by carts.

restrictive line should not incline toward the curving direction... Punishment should not shun officials and reward should not shun citizens," (*Han Fei Zi, Ruling the Country with Law*). In other words, he thought that law should be equal and fair to everyone, whatever their status. In addition, he thought that law must be publicized among citizens: "Law was compiled in books, made by government, and publicized among citizens," (*Legal System*). Han Fei also stressed that no one could stand above the law, even a ruler: "A wise ruler chooses talents based on the law rather than on his opinion; a wise ruler evaluates officials based on the law rather than on his judgment." (*Ruling the Country with Law*). In short, he thought that law was a norm that possessed universal restrictive power – as he indicated in the following quotation:

**A ruler who practices law effectively will strengthen the country and a ruler who practices law ineffectively will weaken the country. (*Ruling the Country with Law*)**

**If a ruler acts in accordance with law, citizens live in peace and the country enjoys stability; if officials observe law, the country owns a powerful army and the enemy weakens. (*Ruling the Country with Law*)**

Han Fei also contrasted the Qin Kingdom and the Six Kingdoms: "When the law is made clearly, faithful officials are encouraged; when punishment is practiced uncompromisingly, treacherous officials are prohibited. These help to expand the land and enlarge the ruler's influence. The Kingdom of Qin is like that. However, when officials form clique to pursue self-interest, the law is distorted. This helps to lose the land and weaken the ruler's influence. The Six Kingdoms are like that," (*Rectifying Morality*). Meanwhile, Han Fei knew how difficult it was to reform and practice law. He noted: "Therefore, if one who knows tactics and law is appointed, the powerful officials must be punished by law. In this sense, one who practices law is an implacable enemy to the powerful officials," (*Lonely Indignation*). In addition, he noted that reformers often ended miserably: "When the reformers cannot win against the corrupted officials, there will be two opposite forces. How can the reformers not exist in danger? If the reformers can be framed with a crime, they will be killed by the law; if not, they will be killed by the sword secretly," (*Lonely Indignation*). Examples of this include Shang Yang being turned asunder by five carts and Wu Qi being killed with arrow. Although he was aware of threats such as these, we can sense Han Fei's firm determination and noble spirit[25].

In addition to the law, Legalism also discussed political trickery. Han Fei commented, "A ruler who cannot master political trickery will be deceived and officials who do not observe the law will commit crimes... A ruler should master both law and political trickery," (*Making Law*). In other words he was saying that political trickery and the law were complementary. So what exactly is political trickery? Han Fei defined it in the following way: "Political trickery hides in the heart of a ruler, and is the way in which the ruler controls the officials secretly," (*Legal System*). For Han Fei, a prominent feature of political trickery was hiding or masking one's feelings. He explained this as follows: "[a ruler can] hide his likes and dislikes, thoughts, wisdom and talents so that officials

---

25. It should be added that the reforms carried out by Legalists resulted in some remarkable achievements and embodied the strong color of *Gong* (the public). Many philosophers highly praised Legalism. For instance, Liu Zongyuan commented, "the Kingdom of Qin abolished the enfeoffment system. That's a great step forward although it aimed to reinforce the ruler's power and conquer others. However, the idea that the country belonged to all started from the Kingdom of Qin," (*On Enfeoffment System*).

Han Fei (280-233 BC), also known as Han Fei Zi, was born in the Kingdom of Han during the late Warring States Period. He was a representative philosopher of Legalism.

cannot understand what he really thinks and what he really means," (*The Ruler's Law*). Clearly, political trickery was a tool for the exercise of a ruler's despotism. In China, it was called Facing-South Trickery. To sum up, political trickery was mysterious, hidden and insidious. Political trickery was certainly the lowest of the ideas of Han Fei or Legalism. However, it represented the social reality of the time and was therefore necessary[26].

The ideas of Legalism exerted profound influence on Chinese history. First, during the Warring States period, it was not the influence of Confucianism but Legalism that led to the prosperity of the Kingdom of Qin. In particular, Han Fei's idea of "rule by law" helped King Zheng of Qin to unify China. This suggested that a country that practiced the idea of the rule by law in a limited way, would became stronger than a country that did not[27]. Second, in the 2,000-year history of Chinese politics, the principle for ruling has been either "Confucianism in use and Legalism as the base" or the "Co-existence of Confucianism and Legalism" or "Confucianism in use and Political Trickery as the base." In the last of these political trickery had been fully accepted, but the spirit of law contained in Legalism had not been embodied.

---

26. In Europe, Machiavelli also stressed that it would be considered reasonable to play tricks, deceive, act insincerely, tell lies, use violence, and break one's faith as long as this favored the ruler.

27. We must note that the law in Legalism was made by the ruler and that it emphasized punishment. This was very different from the laws made in the parliament or General Assembly in ancient Greece and Rome.

# Views on History

The way in which Chinese Philosophers viewed history was an important part of the way in which they viewed society. Among the various views on history held in ancient China, the Confucian view was the most influential. In addition, the circulatory theory of history played an important role in ancient China and presented itself in a diverse number of forms.

## Various Views on History

China boasts a long history, during which various views on history have been nurtured. In particular, in the Pre-Qin era when free speech was allowed, the various views on history were a part of the Contention of a Hundred Schools of Thought. Among them, the Confucian view on history was the most important as it dominated China for nearly 2,000 years.

The Confucian view on history was that of the sage and ruler. It claimed that history recorded the deeds of heroes or rulers, and that history was determined by the few. Confucius liked following Yao and Shun. In *The Analects*, Confucius said,

> **It was so great that Shun and Yu did not rule the country by usurpation.**
>
> **Shun stands as lofty as mountain. The heaven is the greatest and Shun is following the heaven.** (*Tai Bo*)

Confucius also extolled the Zhou Dynasty, "The morality in the Zhou Dynasty can be the greatest Morality," (*Tai Bo*). Later, Mencius proposed to follow the early kings (Yao and Shun) and

Xun Zi proposed to follow the late kings (King Wen and King Wu). Different as they seemed, they were same in that they both followed tradition, although in different degrees.

The Confucian view on history was also a "classic" view. This meant that for Confucians history recorded experience or tradition. It also embodied the conservative stance, which worshipped the past and "denied" the present. It was said that Confucius deleted the *Book of Documents and Classic of Poetry*, edited the *Book of Etiquette and Rites* and *Classic of Music*, expounded *Commentaries on Book of Change* and compiled the Spring and Autumn Annals (collectively called the Six Classics). However, this is not credible. In fact, Confucianism was the dominant school of thought in China after the Han Dynasty and it practiced the principle of "rejecting the other schools of thought and respecting only Confucianism." As a result, the books in *San Dai* (Xia, Shang, and Zhou dynasties) were worshipped as Confucian classics (these included *Five Classics, Nine Classics* and *Eleven Classics to Thirteen Classics*). Through this process, the view of history that valued classical tradition was gradually cultivated in China (this was fundamentally destroyed in the modern Chinese era for various reasons).

Alongside Confucianism, Mohism was another school of thought that valued tradition but it took the Xia Dynasty as its model. Taoism admired the primitive societies of ancient times but did not worship the sage. Legalism held a unique and clear view on history: its adherents worshiped the present and denied the past. Han Fei's view is an example of this:

> **In the Zhou Dynasty, man vied with morality; in the Spring and Autumn Period, man vied with strategy; now, man vies with force. (*Han Fei Zi, Five Kinds of Vermin*)**

> **Therefore, a sage does not learn all from the past and follow the unalterable law. He takes strategy in accordance with the present condition. (*Han Fei Zi, Five Kinds of Vermin*)**

These quotations show that Han Fei thought that way a ruler should rule should change according to the times. Like Shang Yang, Han Fei viewed history as changeable and evolutionary. In the history of Chinese thought, Legalism has been given less attention than Confucianism; however, its view that the old should be reformed and that the new should be pursued inspired many philosophers to develop a reforming spirit. In addition, as the political trickery of Legalism was embraced by rulers, this reforming spirit had a significant impact on many Confucian scholars.

There are some other important issues relating to how Chinese philosophers viewed history that should be noted.

Confucianism attributed the rationality of a ruler to the will or order of heaven, an approach known as the Divine-right Theory of Kingship. In other words, he thought that those things that were predestined by heaven were reasonable. In fact, this theory was established as early as the Shang and Zhou dynasties. Later, Dong Zhongshu summarized it into a philosophical view: "The heaven remains steady, so will Tao," (*History of Han Dynasty, Biography of Dong Zhongshu*). In

Stone Inscriptions of *Thirteen Classics* (Stone Inscriptions of Emperor Qianlong) in the Confucius Temple in Beijing. *Thirteen Classics* refers to the thirteen Confucian classics (which contain 630,000 words). These included the *Book of Change*, the *Book of Documents*, the *Book of Songs*, the *Rites of Zhou Dynasty*, the *Book of Ceremony*, the *Book of Rites, Zuo Zhuan*, the *Commentary of Gongyang,* the *Commentary of Gulian*g, *The Analects, Er Ya*, the *Classic of Filial Piety* and *Mencius*. There were 190 stelles in total. They were originally placed in front of the Six Halls of the Imperial College to facilitate teaching and learning. Due to the renovation of the Imperial College, they were moved to the corridor between the Imperial College and the Confucius Temple.

Chinese Characters *Tian Xia Wei Gong* (What is under heaven is for all), written by Sun Yat-sen, part of the collection of the National Museum of China.

the meantime, Confucianism realized that heaven's order was not necessarily given to the ruler. In the Zhou Dynasty, this view was deeply understood:

> **He (the king) is no more credible to the Heaven and cannot maintain the Heaven's order long. (*Jun Shi*)**
>
> **There is no ruler who can worship the heaven forever; there is no official who can serve the ruler forever.**

Therefore, it was thought that a ruler must bear a sense of crisis (as the Duke of Zhou had discussed). In the *Commentaries on Book of Change*, this idea was summarized as: "A gentleman must remind himself of danger when in safety, remind himself of fall when in rise, remind himself of disturbance when in peace, so that he can remain safe and a country can enjoy peace," (*Xi Ci II*).

In addition, the Confucianism of the late Warring States Period considered the different types (or stages) of human society. In the *Book of Rites*, there were two indifferent types of human society: the Great Unity Society (*Da Tong*, a utopian vision of the world in which everyone and everything is at peace) and the Basically Well-off Society (*Xiao Kang*, in which people are able to live relatively comfortably). In *Li Yun* of *Book of Rites*, the Great Unity Society was considered to be the ideal society. Utopian as it seemed, it had positive impact on many progressive thinkers.

In the later stages of ancient Chinese philosophy, Wang Fuzhi's view on history was the most valuable. Wang Fuzhi proposed the ideas *Li* and *Shi*. He believed that *Li* and *Shi* determined the development of history. *Li* stood for "rule" and *Shi* for "trend". He said: "When *Shi* becomes inevitable, it turns to *Li*; when *Li* becomes natural, it turns to *Shi*," (*Reading the Four Classics, Li Lou I*). Wang Fuzhi's view revealed deep truths about the unity of law and trend, which led to a better understanding of historical development.

## The Circulatory Theory of History

Meanwhile, ancient Chinese views on history were heavily influenced by circulatory theory, which was widely accepted by many schools of thought. It should be noted that the circulatory theory of history was supported by what was seen in the heavens – the circulatory movement of the celestial bodies, including the changes of the four seasons, the waxing and waning of the moon, the rise and fall of the sun, the cycle of the *Five Star*, etc. The circulatory theory of history was also reflected in the thoughts of Lao Tzu, for instance:

> **It exists forever without any support of the external force; it moves circularly and ceaselessly.**
>
> **When one thing reaches the highest level, it will fade; when it fades, it will develop in the opposite direction.**
>
> **To develop in the opposite direction means the movement of Tao.**

The View of the Five Elements could be also understood as a view on the heavens (no matter scientific or mysterious), which laid a solid foundation for the circulatory theory of history.

The earliest and most representative form of the circulatory theory of history was the Theory of the Start and End of the Five Virtues. This was proposed by Zou Yan in the late Warring States Period. According to this theory, one virtue (one Element of the Five Elements) determined a dynasty's fate, with the progression of dynasties following the order of the Five Virtues (the Five Elements). Zou Yan's thought was embodied in *The Annals of Lü Buwei*:

Shao Yong, from *Portraits of Famous Officials in History*. Shao Yong (1011-1077) was also known as Shao Yaofu and Mr. Anle. His ancestral home was in Fanyang, Hebei Province. He was a famous philosopher, a scholar of the *Book of Change*, and a scholar of the School of Mind.

> **Before a ruler or king appears, heaven must show the people a sign. For the Yellow Emperor, heaven showed a huge earthworm and a mole cricket, and Yellow Emperor said, "Earth rose." As the earth looked yellow, yellow was worshipped. For Yu, heaven showed thriving grass in winter, and Yu said, "Wood rose." As wood looked green, green was valued. For Tang, heaven showed a sword in water, and Tang said, "Metal rose." As the sword looked white, so white was chosen. For King Wen, heaven showed a raven with a red script in its mouth standing above the ancestral temple, and King Wen said, "Fire rose." As fire looked red, red was respected. What would replace fire must be water and the heaven showed a scene of water. As water rose, black was worshiped. When water ended, earth re-appeared. (*Ying Tong*)**

In fact, the circulatory theory of history was ingrained in Chinese thought. For instance, Mencius said, "A new ruler will arise within 500 years," (*Mencius, Gong Sun*

*Chou II*). Mencius also argued, "From Yao and Shun to Tang, there was over 500 years… From Tang to King Wen, there was also over 500 years… From King Wen to Confucius, there was 500 years too… From Confucius to the present, there was more than 100 years, so there is no sage now," (*With All Heart II*). Here Mencius is indicating that history was determined by heroes, and that the circulatory nature of history could be sensed. Later, Dong Zhongshu proposed the theories of "San Tong" and "San Zheng" in *Luxuriant Dew of the Spring and Autumn Annals* (*Chun Qiu Fan Lu*). The theory of *San Tong* referred to the tradition of three colors - black, white, and red. To Dong Zhongshu, the Xia, Shang, and Zhou dynasties changed in accordance with the order of the three colors. The theory of *San Zheng* referred to the three first-months. In this theory, the Xia Dynasty took the month of *Yin* (January in the lunar calendar) as its first month, The Shang Dynasty took the month of *Chou* (December in the lunar calendar) as its first, and the Zhou Dynasty took the month of *Zi* (November in the lunar calendar) as its first. In this view, when a new dynasty was established, the first month of the year and the color of clothes must be changed. It was noticeable that Dong Zhongshu's theory was affected by Zou Yan's Theory of the Start and End of the Five Virtues. In the long history of China, the theories of *San Tong* and *San Zheng* played a pivotal role in the foundation of dynasties. It even had an impact on the slogan of the peasant's uprising: "Yellow Turbans Uprising in Eastern Han Dynasty: Black-Heaven Has Already Died, and Yellow-Heaven Will Set Up".

Afterwards, Shao Yong, a philosopher during the Northern Song Dynasty, proposed the Theory of *Yuan*, *Hui*, *Yun*, and *Shi* in *Imperial Calendar of Dynasties* (*Huang Ji Jing Shi*). Shao Yong applied the theory of Heavenly Stems and Earthly Branches and concluded that 30 years was one *Shi*, 12 *Shi* was one *Yun*, 30 *Yun* was one *Hui*, and 12 *Hui* was one *Yuan*, namely, 1 *Yuan* = 12 *Hui* × 30 *Yun* × 12 *Shi* × 30 years = 129,600 years. According to Shao Yong, one Yuan was a complete cycle, over which time nature would "start and finish". The progression of such cycles was endless.

The philosopher Wang Fuzhi's views also accorded with the circulatory theory of history, but he talked about cycles of peace and disturbance: "The main trend for a country was merely the cycle of division and unification, peace and disturbance," (*My Reading of History as a Mirror*, Vol. 16). Wang Fuzhi's view demystified the circulatory theory of history and embodied a more objective approach to the understanding of historical cycles.

# WHAT IS THE PROPER ORIENTATION OF LIFE?

What is the proper orientation of life? Philosophers in ancient China expressed a range of diverse and valuable views on this important question. For Confucians, the proper orientation of life was embodied by an ideal character, who was called sage or gentleman (*Jun Zi*), which in Confucian terms mean "a perfect man". Ethically, the proper orientation of life was thought of in terms of morality or an ideal (i.e. the ethical basis for being a sage). Anthropologically, the proper orientation of life referred to the "ideal model" that epitomized this morality or ideal. It was perceived that the proper orientation of life related to how a person behaved or the kind of character they chose (i.e. the guidelines that a person lived by). Confucius provided the basic guidelines for how to cultivate an ideal character. Meanwhile, Confucian thinkers concerned themselves with human nature, not only with respect to goodness and evil but also with respect to the cultivation of individual morality and social fashion. For example, Mencius's thought that human nature was good and Xun Zi thought that human nature was bad. Taoism put forward different opinions on the proper orientation of life. For example, Lao Tzu and Chuang Tzu were inclined to see it as an attitude or manner of living – in other words, an outlook on life.

# The Ideal Confucian Character and Its Cultivation

Confucians held the ideal that one should possess the sage's virtue and practice the ruler's policy. The latter issue was discussed was discussed in Chapter 3, and it was also mentioned in relation to the Eight Terms (*Ba Tiao Mu*) in *Great Learning*: to regulate the family, to maintain the state rightly and to make all peaceful. Practicing the ruler's policy was, in fact, linked to the idea of the sage's virtue, which was mentioned in *Great Learning* as being about "cultivating morality" (*Xiu Shen*) and as comprising righteousness and sincerity. *Great Learning* began with: "The great learning teaches to act in accordance with morality (*Ming De*), to respect citizens, and to maintain the perfectness," (*Zhi Shan*). Here, Ming De and Zhi Shan are referring to the ideal cultivation of morality, which would lead to the development of an ideal human character. Actually, the idea of the ideal character was first established in the Confucianism of Pre-Qin times.

## The Ideal Confucian Character Established by Confucius

The ideal Confucian character consisted of the following principles (which were mainly established by Confucius):

One: *Tao* and Righteousness. These principles mainly centered on righteousness and profit and included three rules.

**1.** Righteousness is the most important principle of the ideal character. Confucius said, "A gentleman gives priority (*Shang*) to righteousness," (*The Analects, Yang Huo*). Here,

*Shang* meant "the first place." Xun Zi elaborated on this idea further, "A gentleman can be insulted by power but not by the loss of Righteousness," (*Xun Zi, On Righteousness*). *Tao* and Righteousness were so important that Confucius said, "I can die in the dusk as long as I know what *Tao* means in the morning," (*The Analects, Li Ren*).

2. Value righteousness and underestimate profit. The edict that "righteousness is the most important" also meant that "profit has the least importance." Confucius said, "I remind myself of righteousness when facing profit," (*Xian Wen*) and "It is meaningless to me when I obtain wealth and power but act against righteousness," (*Shu Er*). However, Mencius overstated the value of righteousness, "It is unnecessary to mention profit as there is only benevolence and righteousness," (*Mencius, King Hui of Liang I*).

3. Be satisfied with poverty and devoted to *Tao*. This rule indicated how a person should act in the face of poverty. Confucius stressed, "Wealth and power are what man desires, but he must not enjoy them if he obtains them in an improper manner. Poverty and humanness are what man dislikes, but he must not abandon them if he abandons them in the wrong way. How should a gentleman be called a gentleman if he discards benevolence? A gentleman cannot live without benevolence even when he has dinner, even when he faces urgency, and even when he suffers homelessness." (*Li Ren*) Confucius took Yan Hui, his disciple, as an example: "Yan Hui, so virtuous! He lives with a bamboo dish of rice and a gourd of drink in a remote lane. When others worry him, he does not change his devotion. Yan Hui, so virtuous! (*Yong Ye*)." Here, Confucianism places the gentleman in opposition to the petty man.

Two: The principle for ideal. This was mainly based on moralism and included four rules.

1. Improving oneself. This rule stated that a man should follow the rule "improve oneself" when faced with the goodness and evil (in the same way that he should follow the rule "satisfied with poverty and devoted to *Tao*" in the face of poverty). Confucius said, "One should serve the ruler when Tao is practiced and seclude oneself when *Tao* is not practiced," (*Tai Bo*) and "One should take a small raft and live a secluded life when *Tao* is not practiced," (*Gong Ye Chang*). Mencius also stated, "In poverty, one should maintain one's integrity; when on the rise, one should make perfect the whole country," (*With All Heart I*).

**2.** Adhere to goodness. This rule highlighted the importance of upholding the truth, as Confucius said, "One should adhere to benevolence and even surpass his teacher," (*King Ling of Wei*) and "One should be devoted to honesty, learning, and goodness with whole heart," (*Tai Bo*).

**3.** Maintain integrity. Confucius said, "One can carry off the commander from a whole army, but cannot take away the will of the common folk," (*Zi Han*). Zeng Sen said, "Could a man be called a gentleman, to whom a ruler can entrust his young successor and the whole country, who does not change his will in the face of peril? Yes, he must be a gentleman," (*Tai Bo*).

**4.** Devote your life to *Tao*. The final rule was to devote one's life to *Tao*. Confucius said, "One with "ideal" sacrifices himself to practice benevolence rather than harm benevolence for his survival," (*King Ling of Wei*). Mencius said, "One with "ideal" does not fear if he is deserted in the wild; one with valor does not fear if he is killed," (*Duke of Wen of Teng II*) and "One should devote himself to Tao when Tao is not practiced," (*With All Heart I*). This rule elevated Confucian morality to the highest level, as it called for the highest and most noble of sacrifices.

Three: The principle of perfection. This included three rules:

**1.** Strive for honesty and tolerance. This rule was the embodiment of the spirit of benevolence and highlighted the importance of taking others into account. It had two implications: "One cannot give what he dislikes to others," (*King Ling of Wei*) and "One who bears benevolence to others will obtain benevolence from others; one who bears tolerance to others will obtain tolerance from others," (*Yong Ye*). This meant that a man should not require others to achieve what he could not achieve himself[28] and that he should extend the morality he practiced to others. In fact, the rule had multiple meanings. These included: "be

---

28. In an international conference on religion held in Chicago in 1993, the principle that one cannot give what one dislikes to others (which was expressed differently in different religions and by different peoples but which had the same meaning) was established as the golden rule for the relationships between different races.

strict with yourself and tolerant to others", "put yourself in the position of others", and "think of others as well as yourself".

2. Strive for the Golden Mean. This idea was discussed in Chapter 2. With respect to the ideal character, Confucius stressed that: "Golden Mean was the greatest virtue!" (*Yong Ye*). He also stated that: "I shall make acquaintance with these who are unruly and upright when I cannot find one who practices Golden Mean. The unruly does all he wants and the upright refuses to do something," (*Zi Lu*). Meanwhile, Confucius suggested that a man who practices the Golden Mean would be thought of as a "fence-straddler" or *Xiang Yuan*. (Note: *The original sentence in The Analects* said a *Xiang Yuan* who did not offend anyone or distinguish good or evil was a "theft of morality.")

3. Strive for Maturity. By maturity, this rule meant the unity of truth, goodness and beauty, or the unity of ideas, emotions and will. Confucius said, "One's cultivation starts from the learning of poetry, develops in the learning of rite, and ends in the learning of music," (*Tai Bo*). Xun Zi further noted that: "A gentleman views what he learns incompletely or inexactly as imperfect," (*Encouraging Learning*). These statements look at the ideal character from the

*Three Confucian Sages*, by Zhao Mengfu in Yuan Dynasty. In the middle is Confucius. Yan Hui is on the left and Zeng Shen on the right, both are listening to Confucius. There are lines from *The Analects* in their clothes. These are written in regular script in small characters.

Inside the Hall of Honesty and Tolerance, in the Kong Family Mansion, Qufu, Shandong Province. The Hall of Honesty and Tolerance was inspired by the line that a gentleman should be honest and tolerant. It was the place where Confucius' descendents learnt poetry and rite.

perspective of perfectness. (The issues of emotion and beauty are discussed later.)

Four: The Principle of self-discipline. To Confucians, morality could not be imposed on human with laws or force. Confucius said, "One should not expect others to practice benevolence except oneself," (*Yan Yuan*). Mencius said, "One should act in accordance with benevolence rather than practice benevolence for benevolence's sake," (*Li Lou II*). This principle included four rules:

1. Demand goodness of oneself. Confucius said, "A Gentleman demands of himself while a petty man demands of others," (*King Ling of Wei*). Mencius said, "To practice benevolence is like shooting. The shooter stands correctly before he shoots. If he fails to hit the target, he should examine himself rather than complain about one who beats him," (*Gong Sun Chou I*).

2. Practice self-examination. Confucius said, "When one sees a man of worth, he should think of equaling him; when one sees a man of a contrary character, he should turn inwards and examine himself," (*Li Ren*). Zeng Sen, a disciple of Confucius, said, "I examine myself three times a day: Am I unfaithful when I give suggestions to others? Am I dishonest when I make friends with others? Do I review what I learn?" (*Xue Er*)

3. Correct one's mistakes. This rules highlights the idea that what matters is not whether a man makes mistakes but whether he realizes the fact and corrects them. Confucius said, "If one has made mistakes, he should not fear to correct it," (*Xue Er*). and "It is a mistake if one does not correct his mistake," (*King Ling of Wei*).

4. Restrain oneself in privacy. In the *Doctrine of the Mean*, it was mentioned that: "A gentleman must be cautious where others do not see or hear him. There is no privacy that cannot be discovered and no trivia that cannot be exposed. Therefore, a gentleman restrains himself in privacy." This highlighted the idea that self-discipline was different from discipline imposed by others which was fulfilled by order and was close to ethic. Instead, self-discipline depended on self-examination and was close to morality[29].

The ideal Confucian character – as established by Confucius – presents us with a spirit of uprightness, loftiness and indomitability. This ideal has provided spiritual support to Chinese civilization since ancient times. It has guided the country, become the soul of its people, and deeply affected its society and history. In fact, many great philosophers have assumed the responsibility that comes with living to this ideal. For instance, Mencius said, "Today, except me, who can make the whole country peaceful?" (*Gong Sun Chou II*). Zhang Zai stated, "I would like to learn all knowledge, to serve people, to inherit the thoughts of sages, and to create a peaceful world for the future," (*Quotations from Zhang Zi*). These philosophers actually embodied the ideal that one should possess the sage's virtue and practice the ruler's policy. We must note that the ideal Confucian character presented strong *Jun Zi* (or in other words had a elitist sensibility). This meant that the officials (*Jun Zi*) who advocated and cultivated morality excluded common citizens (*Xiao Ren*)[30]. (Note: Here the words *Jun Zi* and *Xiao Ren* referred to people with high or low status. They

---

29. In the ethics of the Abrahamic religions, the ethic of Protestantism seems closest to self-discipline. In Western philosophy and ethics, Kant's view is very similar to the Confucian view: "Morality expresses nothing but pure and practical self-discipline, or self-discipline in freedom." Kant, Critique of Practical Reason. Beijing: Commercial Press, 1999, pp. 34-35.

30. Compared with the more universal care espoused by the Abrahamic religions, Confucian view was flawed, as Max Weber expounded.

were different from the terms "gentleman" and "petty man" who were different in morality.) This view on the cultivation of morality was not changed until in the Song Dynasty, as seen in "Edification and the ethical tradition of the Chinese civilization."

## The Cultivation of the Ideal Character

Confucians not only elucidated the features of the ideal character but also expressed their views on its cultivation. This included two main aspects.

One: The integrity and unity of reason. Here the term "reason" encompasses knowledge and morality, or truth and goodness. In Confucianism these ideas were called wisdom (*Zhi*) and benevolence (*Shan*) respectively.

Confucius was the first to unify wisdom and benevolence. In *The Analects*, wisdom and benevolence were often mentioned at the same time:

> **Fan Chi asked what benevolence was. Confucius said, "Love others." Fan Chi asked what wisdom was. Confucius said, "Know others." (*Yan Yuan*)**

> **Confucius said, "A kind man is satisfied with benevolence and a wise man is beneficial to benevolence." (*Li Ren*)**

Why did Confucius mention benevolence and wisdom together? It was because, for him, they were the embodiment of the consciousness of reason. To Confucius, benevolence meant *Tao* or truth, while wisdom meant to pursue *Tao* or truth. Benevolence or *Tao* was put in first place, which indicated the value Confucius placed on morality or the understanding of truth. Meantime, benevolence was understood through wisdom. Indeed, it was thought that without wisdom benevolence did not have real meaning. For instance:

**Hear, and then choose the good to learn; see, and then remember in heart. (*Shu Er*)**

**I choose the goodness in him to learn and correct my demerit when I see his. (*Shu Er*)**

In some sense, Confucius was the first to unify truth and goodness and knowledge and morality, as well as epistemology, methodology and ethnics. In addition, in Confucianism, the unity of virtue and wisdom was embodied not only through the unity of benevolence and wisdom, but also through the unity of righteousness and wisdom. This indicates Confucianism's deep understanding of *Tao* and benevolence, or righteousness and profit, and its understanding of how to make the right choice between them. For instance, Mencius stated that: "Life is what I desire; righteousness is also what I desire. When I cannot obtain both, I sacrifice life for righteousness," (*Gao Zi I*).

Two: The Cultivation of ideal and courage. Confucius emphasized the importance of setting up one's ideal: "When I was fifteen, I took learning as my ideal," (*Wei Zheng*). Here, Confucius is saying that he decided to devote himself to benevolence and Tao at the age of fifteen.

*Confucius Teaching Zi Lu Benevolence, Anecdotes Collected from the Spring and Autumn Period to Han Dynasty, Vol. 1, Masterpieces in the Prosperous Time.*

Akin to Confucius, Mencius highlighted the role that an ideal played in the cultivation of the ideal character:

> I can discern one's ideal through his words and can cultivate my noble spirit (*Hao Ran Zhi Qi*)… The noble spirit presents great and grand. If it has been nurtured by uprightness and kept unhurt, it will spread in the heaven and earth. (*Gong Sun Chou I*)
>
> Therefore, if the heaven wants to lay an important task on someone, the heaven must agonize his will, tire his bone, hunger him, and disturb his deeds. (*Gao Zi II*)

To Mencius, the cultivation of a person's ideal was the same as the cultivation of their noble spirit and it was arduous work. For him, if a person cultivated their ideal then they would toughen themselves up. He thought that the harder the environment a person faced, the tougher they would become. He also thought that a person's will was closely related to their valor which had to gradually cultivated and accumulated:

> A common man cannot be deprived of his will.
>
> One can sacrifice his life to practice benevolence.
>
> One with an ideal does not fear if he is deserted in the wild; one with valor does not fear if he is killed.

*Mencius* presents us with an image of a true man who stands loftily and who despises powerful men:

> Neither poverty nor humbleness can make him swerve from principle; neither threats nor forces can subdue him. That's what I meant by a true man. (*Duke of Wen of Teng II*)

They are heroes, so am I. Why must I fear them? (*Duke of Wen of Teng II*)

When one speaks to a powerful man, he should despise him and ignore his status and power. (*With All Heart II*)

Xun Zi also expressed a similar view:

Therefore, power cannot subdue him; others cannot change him; things cannot shake him. He remains unchanged, no matter if he lives or dies. That's what I meant by virtue and integrity. (*Encouraging Learning*)

A man can utter or keep silent; a man can defy or yield. However, one cannot change his will. If right, accept; if wrong, refuse. (*Removing Obstructions*)

These philosophers advised that a person should never yield to the powerful and the noble and that they should adhere to their ideals and keep their integrity. Through the words of Confucius, Mencius, and Xun Zi, we clearly see how the ideal Confucian character continued to be improved.

# Music and Character Building

In addition to reason and will, emotions also played a part in the traditional Confucian ideal character. It was thought that normal and commendable emotions often embodied normal and commendable virtues. Then, how could such emotions be cultivated? Confucianism believed that music played a crucial role.

## Completion through Music

The value that Confucianism placed on music was deeply influenced by the rite or culture of the Zhou Dynasty. Confucius said, "To enlighten with poetry, to educate with rite, and to complete with music," (*The Analects, Tai Bo*). In other words, "completion through music" was the highest stage in the cultivation of character. Confucius himself benefited a lot from music:

> **Since Shi Zhi starts to play, my ears have been pleased until he ends with *Crying Ospreys*. (*Tai Bo*)**

> **It was recorded that after Confucius heard *Shao* music, he did not know how meat tasted for a long time and said, "I do not think I am so fascinated with music like that." (*Shu Er*)**

It was thought by Confucians that one could achieve a "great state" by cultivating one's aesthetics and emotions. In Xian Jin, it was recorded that Confucius asked his disciples to tell him their ideals. Zi Lu, Ran Qiu, Gong Chixi said theirs, then it was Zeng Dian's turn. Confucius said,

"Dian, how about yours?" Zeng Dian answered, "In late spring, the clothes are finished. I take a bath in the Yishui River with more than ten adults and youths and I feel the spring wind at the Terrace for Praying Rain. Then we sing and return." Confucius nodded and said, "That's also what I want!" Zeng Dian did not confine his ideas to reality and presented a romantic and pleasant spirit. It was so beautiful and it also put across a feeling of real human pleasure.

Subsequently, the book the *Theory on Music* and *Record on the Subject of Music* elaborated on the role music played in the cultivation of character. The *Theory on Music* was written by Xun Zi. In the *Theory on Music*, it was clearly stated that, "Music is what expresses pleasure; the musical instruments made with metal and bamboo are what indicate morality." The *Record of Music* inherited the views expressed in the *Theory on Music* and stressed the close relationship between music and morality:

Music relates to morality. (*Nature of Music*)

One who possesses rite and music both embodied morality. (*Nature of Music*)

*Confucius Teaching Rite and Music.* A stone mural in an old temple in Xingcheng, Liaoning Province.

**Music symbolizes morality. (*Play of Music*)**

**Music represents the essence of morality. (*Image of Music*)**

At the same time, the *Theory on Music* and the *Record on the Subject of Music* clearly suggested the significance of music to human emotions:

**Music expresses the human pleasure that all have. (*Theory on Music*)**

**Music comes from one's heart. Sound forms when human emotions are evoked. Music forms when sound is organized. (*Record on the Subject of Music*)**

**Music always expresses one's emotion. (*Emotion in Music*)**

It should be noted that the clarification of the relationship between music and emotion was very important to the authors of these books. This shows that it was thought that the cultivation of character was closely related to emotions and aesthetics, and that a "complete character" must embody both emotions and aesthetics. In addition, the *Theory on Music* and the *Record of Music* both emphasized the role that music could play in the cultivation of a person's character and morality. They also discussed how music could reform people and transform social customs. For instance:

**Music is what a sage likes. It can make citizens kind, move people, and transform social customs. Therefore, the late king guided citizens with music and made them harmonious. (*Theory on Music*)**

**To rule with music can publicize morality, make citizens healthy and peaceful, transform social customs, and bring peace to a country. (*Record on the Subject of Music*)**

> **Therefore, gentlemen harmonize their wills according to their natures and cultivate themselves by popularizing music amongst themselves. A gentleman displays morality when he popularizes music and guides citizens in the right direction. (*Image of Music*)**

This shows that it was thought that music could lead people to do good deeds and fulfill moral goals. In this sense, it was thought that the popularity of music was of enormous importance to the cultivation of character and morality.

## Equilibrium and Harmony

Equilibrium was an important idea in Confucianism. It stood for fairness, properness, harmony, and peace. In fact, equilibrium combined the ideas of the Doctrine of the Mean and Harmony (as discussed in Chapter 2). As a philosophical idea, equilibrium was first recorded in the *Doctrine of the Mean*:

"The Doctrine of the Mean indicates that one's happiness, anger, sorrow, and joy are not expressed; harmony indicates that one's happiness, anger, sorrow, and joy are expressed but in a moderate way. The Doctrine of the Mean is the cardinal principle in the world and harmony is the embodiment of *Tao*. When equilibrium has been achieved, the heaven and earth are in good order, and all are nurtured."

This was the most complete discussion of the idea of Equilibrium in the early Confucian classics. Although this explanation of the idea Doctrine of the Mean might sound unreasonable, an understanding of harmony as equilibrium was sensible – this was also how Confucius understood the nature of the Doctrine of the Mean. Equilibrium definitely embodied a strong moral character, which could be seen from the nature of the Doctrine of the Mean. In addition, equilibrium was an ideal; as the lines above suggest it was, "the cardinal principle in the world," "the embodiment of *Tao*," "the heaven and earth in good order and all nurtured." Generally speaking, the concept of equilibrium was not clearly discussed in *Doctrine of the Mean*. Then, how should we understand it?

Serial bells for rite and music, in Hall of Mental Cultivation of the Palace Museum, Beijing

In fact, equilibrium was, to a large extent, an aesthetic idea, which was closely related to music. The idea therefore developed and matured in the discussions that philosophers had about music. In this sense, we may call equilibrium the beauty of harmony. This raises the question: How were equilibrium and harmony formed and combined in Chinese musical theory?

As mentioned above, the idea Harmony in China was first recorded in the *Book of Documents* and this was in relation to music: "Poetry is the expression of earnest thought; singing is the prolonged utterance of that expression; the notes accompany that utterance, and they are harmonized themselves by the standard-tubes. (In this way) the eight different kinds of musical instruments can be adjusted so that one shall not take from or interfere with another; and spirits and men are brought into harmony," (*Canon of Yao*). Later, in the *Discourses of the States*, there was a dialogue on music between King Jing of Zhou Dynasty, Duke Mu of Shan Kingdom, and Lingzhou Jiu:

> **Duke Mu of Shan Kingdom said, "The bell made by the late king was not larger than *jun* (a tool to measure weight) and heavier than 60 kg. Now, the bell made by Your Majesty cannot sound and does not agree with the scale. Now that the bell sounds disorderly and looks unshapely, what's the use of it except that it harms music and wastes the citizens' wealth?**
>
> **If vision and sound disharmonize, one will feel dazed. Then, he cannot taste the delicious. Then, he cannot maintain the vigor. Then, he cannot remain harmonious with others. Consequently, he will utter irrational words, bear absurd ideas, give inconstant orders, and make wrong rules. (*The Discourse of Zhou II*)**

Here, Duke Mu of Shan Kingdom reiterated the importance of harmony, which helped to form the idea of equilibrium and extended the opinions set out in the *Canon of Yao of Book of Documents*. Meanwhile, he mentioned other ideas such as *Jie* and *Du*, which actually meant moderateness or the inherent rationality of things. Similarly, Lingzhou Jiu said,

> **To rule is similar to playing music. Playing music requires harmony. The Five Notes (*Wu Yin*) make the tone pleasing and the Twelve Temperaments (*Shi Er Lü*) make the sound even.**
>
> **Perfect music means all the instruments are used properly; tone means all the sounds are collected; harmony means all the sounds are coordinated; peace means all the alt and undertones are played in an ordered way.**
>
> **The wiry tone is covered by the vast tone, which sounds unpleasant to ears. It is unequal when it sounds low and tortuous. When the tone is hurt and wealth is wasted, the official in charge of music cannot keep control.**
>
> **If there is harmonious tone, there is increased wealth. The poem that expresses harmony accords with morality and the song that eulogizes harmony accords with temperament. When**

morality and temperament are right, the music can connect the heavens with humans. As a result, the heavenly spirit is peaceful and citizens are obedient. If a ruler gratifies his desire by wasting wealth and tiring citizens, the musical instrument sounds neither harmonious nor legal. This hinders edification, loses the citizens' hearts, and infuriates the heavens. I have not heard this.

Temperament determines the tone and loudness. In the past, the drum uses it to judge whether the sound was harmonious.

That the high and low sounds are played means long harmony.

The heavens and humans communicate with numbers and echo with sound. When numbers and sounds are harmonious, the heavens and humans are coordinated.

Evidently the things that Lingzhou Jiu discussed embodied new ideas, such as moderateness and peace (meaning, in this context, that music should be gentle or moderate). So, in the discourses of Duke Mu of the Shan Kingdom and Lingzhou Jiu, we are introduced to aesthetics ideas that relate to music: harmony, moderateness, rationality, meanness, and peace. These constituted the idea of equilibrium. In other words, the idea of equilibrium was formed through the musical practice and thought of the late Western Zhou Dynasty.

In *Zuo Zhuan*, equilibrium was also embodied in Ji Zha's discussion of music (Ji Zha, Prince of the Kingdom Wu): "A musician played *Song* (Sacrificial Songs). Ji Zha said, "It is so great! It expresses righteousness but does not sound arrogant, it is clever but not tiring, sorrowful but not distressful, pleasurable but not overwhelming, vast but not uncontrolled, welcoming but not greedy, peaceful but not static, smooth but not too quick… The Five Sounds (*Wu Sheng*) are harmonious and the Eight Instruments (*Ba Yin*) are in coordination. The rhythm is well controlled and the instruments are in order. These represent the commonness of the great morality," (*The 29th Year of the Reign of Duke Xiang*). Here, Ji Zha used 14 groups of sentences with the "… but not…" structure, which, in itself, indicated the idea of equilibrium.

In *The 1st Year of the Reign of Duke Zhao*, Yi He, a famous doctor, said, "The late king composed music to control things, so there were the Five Sounds (*Wu Sheng*). The slow and quick

Illustration in *Three Character Classic for Children Learning with Illustrations*: The Eight Different Kinds of Musical Instruments, drawn by Jinzhang Bookstore in the early Republic of China. In the ancient Chinese musical and ritual system, there were eight types of musical instrument, namely, gold, stone, string, wood, earth, leather, gourd, and bamboo. Gold referred to bronze instruments; most were bells and some were *Zheng* and *Nao*. Stone referred to stone instruments; most were *Bian Qing*. String referred to string instruments, like *Zheng* and *Se*. Bamboo referred to bamboo instruments, like *Pai Xiao* and *Chi*. Earth referred to earth instruments, like *Xun*. Wood referred to wooden instruments, like *Zhu*. Gourd referred to gourd-like instruments like *Sheng*. Leather referred to leather instruments, like drums.

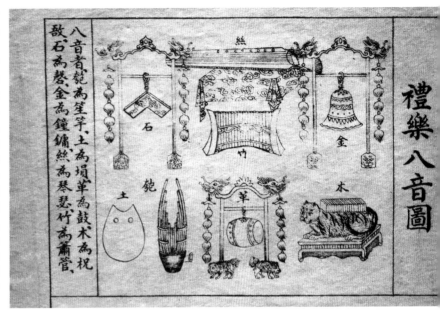

sounds coordinated each other. When the Five Sounds turn to low and stop, one cannot play any longer. Otherwise, it will turn into decadent music. Man will hear restlessness and lewdness and will not be able to remain peaceful, so a gentleman never hears that kind of music." Here Yi He is relating the Five Sounds in music to a person's wellbeing. The Five Sounds referred to *Gong*, *Shang*, *Jiao*, *Zhi*, and *Yu*. In the ancient Chinese seven-tone scale, *Gong*, *Shang*, *Jiao*, *Zhi*, and *Yu* were complete sounds while *Bian Gong* and *Bian Zhi* were half sound. According to *Yi He*, *Gong*, *Shang*, *Jiao*, *Zhi*, and *Yu* were harmonious, whereas *Bian Gong* and *Bian Zhi* were not. It was the disharmony of these notes that caused the "restlessness and lewdness" (*Fan Shou* and *Yin Sheng* in Chinese) he referred to. Yi He also used ideas such as the Doctrine of the Mean, moderateness, peace, and Harmony's View. His thoughts had an enormous impact on ancient Chinese musical theory.

The idea of equilibrium had a direct impact on Confucius. He stated, "*Crying Osprey* sounds joyful but not indecent, sorrowful but not deplorable," (*The Analects, Ba Yi*) and "The music in the

An eight-man band pictured in the mural *Infinite Life Sutra* from the middle Tang Dynasty. In the middle are four dancers on each side, who sit and play. Their instruments are a *Pi- Pa*, a *Sheng*, a *Bi Li*, a *Hai Luo*, clappers, a *Pai Xiao*, a flute, and a clarinet. This mural is located on the south wall of the 20th cave in Yulin Grottoes, Gansu Province.

Kingdom of Zheng is indecent," (*King Ling of Wei*). To Confucius, good music could cultivate a person's temperament and make him kind, while bad music might corrupt public morals and make people evil – which, for him, embodied the idea of equilibrium. Confucius also expressed the idea of equilibrium in a wider way: "Doctrine of the Mean was the greatest virtue!" (*Yong Ye*) and "A gentleman seeks harmony but not uniformity. A petty man seeks uniformity but not harmony."(*Zi Lu*)

Afterwards, the first Chinese book on musicology, the *Theory on Music and Record on the Subject of Music*, took on and developed these thoughts. In the *Record of Music*, it was said:

**The late king made rules in music to restrain the citizens' behavior. (*Nature of Music*)**

**The great music is as harmonious as the heaven and earth; the great rite is as moderate as the heaven and earth. (*Theory on Music*)**

**Music is the harmony between the heaven and earth. (*Theory on Music, Rite of Music*)**

**A gentleman despises the music that destroys equilibrium. (*Language in Music*)**

These remarks suggest the ideas of moderateness, harmony and peace. They also describe equilibrium as a gentleman's virtue. More importantly, both mention music as the "guideline of equilibrium."

"Music is the order of the heaven and earth and the guideline of equilibrium. Humans cannot act against it," (*Edification in Music*). In addition, it was notable that the thoughts in the *Theory on Music and Record of Music* were consistent with the meaning of the *Doctrine of the Mean* described above.

Therefore, equilibrium and harmony became an important part of the cultivation of an ideal character. Certainly, equilibrium and harmony were extended to edification, which was embodied in a similar passage in the *Theory on Music* and the *Record on the Subject of Music*:

Therefore, when music is played in the ancestral temple, the ruler and officials hear and no one shows disrespect; when music is played in a clan, the old and the young hear and no one shows disharmony; when music is played in a family, the father and son hear and no one shows defiance. In accordance, the tone should be firstly decided to coordinate the sound and rhythm should be controlled with instrument. The movement that formed with harmonious tone can harmonize the relationships between the ruler and official, father and son, and win the citizens' support. This is the goal the late king strived to achieve when he made rules in music."[31] (*Edification in Music*)

---

31. Similar views can be seen in *The Annals of Lü Buwei*: "Sound comes from harmony and harmony comes from properness," (*Da Yue*), "Therefore, the task of music is to harmonize heart and to harmonize heart is to act properly," (*Shi Yin*), and "Therefore, a gentleman cultivates his mortality first. Then he composes music. When the music has been harmonious, the country will be peaceful," (*Yin Chu*).

# The Confucian Theory of Human Nature

The consideration of human nature was an indispensable part of the philosophical debate on the proper orientation of life that took place in ancient China. The issue of human nature was discussed as early as the Spring and Autumn Period: "The heaven creates humans and appoints a ruler to manage them, so that they will not lose their nature," (*Zuo Zhuan, The 14<sup>th</sup> Year of the Reign of Duke Xiang*). In addition, the following expressions were used in ancient times: "nature of the petty man" and "nature of the dandy". These associated human nature with goodness and evil (Note: It is hard to equate the Western term *Dandy* with the Chinese term *Gao Liang*. Their similarity, if any, lies in the fact that both refer to a man who was born into a noble family and who lives or pursues a luxurious life.)

**The petty man provokes others due to his reckless courage and makes trouble due to his greed. (*Zuo Zhuan, The 26<sup>th</sup> Year of the Reign of Duke Xiang*)**

**It is the nature of the dandy that is hard to correct. (*Discourses of the States, The Discourse of Jin VII*)**

The Confucian theory of human nature was certainly the most important view held by the multitude of ancient Chinese scholars (and their schools of thoughts). It is thought that Confucius himself did not discuss human nature in a profound way. In *The Analects*, there was only one record of Confucius' view on human nature: "Human beings are born with a similar nature, but their habits make them different," (*Yang Huo*). Confucius's neglect of human nature was confirmed by his disciples. Zi Gong said, "I seldom hear my teacher talking about human nature and *Tao*," (*Gong Ye Chang*). However, in 1993 an article entitled *Human Nature Was Predestined* was found among some bamboo slips unearthed in Guodian, Jingmen, Hubei Province. According to scholars, this was a Confucian article. However, out of all of the Confucian theories on human nature, Mencius'

doctrine of the goodness of human nature and Xun Zi's doctrine of the evil of human nature were the most representative. They embodied the highest level of philosophical thought of their time and exerted profound influence on future theories of human nature.

## Mencius' Doctrine of the Goodness of Human Nature

Mencius' doctrine of the goodness of human nature is widely known among the Chinese. The *Three Character Classic*, a rudimentary book for learning Chinese characters, begins with the line "Human beings are born with a kind nature." For a long time, this line had been a self-evident truth and a basic belief of the Chinese people.

As a theory, Mencius' doctrine of the goodness of human nature developed from Mencius' refutation of Gao Zi's views on human nature. For Mencius, Gao Zi's views on human nature consisted of three key points: That the desire for food and beauty was part of human nature; that human nature was congenital; and that human nature was neutral. Reasonable as Gao Zi's views seem, Mencius thought they had a fateful defect, this was that Gao Zi understood human nature as a natural character or an animal instinct and therefore equated humans with animals, a stance which was refuted by Mencius. He argued against Gao Zi's view that human nature was congenital and said, "Is the nature of a dog the same as that of cattle? Is the nature of cattle the same as that of humans? (*Mencius, Gao Zi I*)." So how did Mencius understand human nature? He proposed the famous theory of "Four Origins" (*Si Duan*) and stated that the "Four Origins" were inborn rather than obtained postnatally:

**All can feel sympathy for others; all can feel shameful; all can show respect; and all can judge right or wrong. The sympathy they express means benevolence; the shame they feel means righteousness; the respect they show means rite; and the judgment they make means wisdom. The four are not given by others but inherent in humans. Humans just do not think and pursue them. (*Mencius, Gao Zi I*)**

Mencius gave an example of his theory in the following way: "All feel sympathy for a child falling in a well and help him," (*Gong Sun Chou I*). For him, this feeling of sympathy, or what he called *Ce Yin*, constituted the basic morality of all humans, also known as "conscience" or "instinctive ability". Mencius stressed that a person who did not possess the "Four Origins" could not be called a human: "One cannot be called a human if one does not feel sympathy for others, does not feel shameful, does not show respect, and does not judge right or wrong," (*Gong Sun Chou I*). Obviously, Mencius took morality, rather than animal-like instinct as Gao Zi did, as the basis of human nature. This was the essence of Mencius' doctrine of the goodness of human nature. Its significance lies in the way it distinguished humans from animals in a fundamental way.

This raised the question as to whether animal-like instincts or desires were embodied in human nature. In fact, Mencius did not completely deny that this type of desire was present in humans: "What mouth was meant to taste was what eyes were meant to form, what ears to sound, what nose to smell, the limbs to comfort. It was human's nature to like them, but it was Destiny that determined. Therefore, a gentleman seldom overstated human nature. What benevolence meant to father and son was what righteousness meant to the ruler and officials, what rite meant to the host and guest, what wisdom meant to the wise man, and what sage meant to

*Portrait of Mencius*, preserved in the Hall of South Fragrance of the Palace Museum, Beijing. Mencius (372-289BC) , who was also known as Meng Ke, was born in Zou (today Zoucheng City, Shandong Province). He was a great philosopher and the main representative of Confucianism in the Warring States Period.

Tao. Whether one can obtain them was determined by the Heaven. Therefore, a gentleman seldom overstated Destiny." (*With All Heart I*). Mencius thaought that one should entrust Destiny with issues of sensory gratification and desire that were not necessarily achieved through human nature; however, he thought that one must not entrust Destiny with issues of righteousness and morality that must be achieved even at the cost of one's life. For Mencius these were the things that really embodied human nature.

Accordingly, Mencius' doctrine of the goodness of human nature put forward the concept of "moral appeal and reflection," which Mencius called "Self-Examination": "When one is dissatisfied with his action, he should examine himself," (*Li Lou I*). The idea of "Self-Examination" was influenced by the view that the "Four Origins" were an inherent part of human nature. In turn it was thought that a person's attitude towards "moral appeal and reflection" would determine the extent to which they achieved moral consciousness. Mencius said, "There is little difference between humans and animals… (Shun) acted in accordance with benevolence rather than practicing benevolence for its sake," (*Li Lou II*). Here, Mencius claimed that the difference between humans and animals lay in the morality that humans possess. He thought that the essence of morality meant that a person not only acts in accordance with social norms but also realizes and obeys the most important values voluntarily[32]. In addition, Mencius thought that anyone could become a sage provided that he improved himself and achieved things: "All can become a sage like Yao and Shun," (*Gao Zi II*). Because of their great profundity, Mencius' thoughts enormously influenced the Lu-Wang School of Mind. They also deserve our consideration today.

Admittedly, there was theoretical defect in Mencius' doctrine of the goodness of human nature: he identified human nature with morality and excluded people's natural attributes. This omission was criticized by Xun Zi.

---

32. In the history of Western philosophy, Kant proposed a similar view to Mencius more than 2,000 years later. Kant said, "It is not enough to justify a good deed using moral criteria. It must be done with moral purposes." This became the core idea in Kantian ethics. Kant, *Fundamental Principles of the Metaphysic of Morals.* Shanghai: Shanghai People's Publishing House, 1986, p. 38.

## Xun Zi's Doctrine of the Evil of Human Nature

Xun Zi's doctrine of the evil of human nature is well known in the history of Chinese thought. Xun Zi disagreed with Mencius' doctrine of the goodness of human nature. He wrote an article entitled On the *Evil of Human Nature* to refute what Mencius had said: "Mencius says human nature is good. I say he is wrong. In history, goodness results from right rule and theory and evil results from danger and disorder. This is the difference between goodness and evil. If human beings are born good, why is there right rule and theory? Why are there wise rulers? Why are there social norms? Why is there right rule and theory since there are wise rulers and social norms?" Through this kind of thinking Xun Zi discovered the theoretical defect in Mencius' approach. For Xun Zi, if human beings were born good there would be no right rule and theory, no wise rulers, and no social norms. Rather, the existence of laws, rite and rulers in a country proved that human nature was evil.

Xun Zi (313-238 BC) was also known as Xun Kuang and Xun Qing. He was a philosopher and educator and the representative of Confucianism in the Warring States Period.

In Xun Zi's view, Mencius did not understand the difference between *Xing* (the natural state or instinctive desire) and *Wei* (humaneness or morality), two qualities that he clearly differentiated.

What was *Xing*? Xun Zi defined it in this way: "*Xing* means the natural state when things come into being." "Xing means the state when things remain unchanged," (*Xun Zi, Rectifying Names*). In other words, *Xing* was the natural state of human nature. Xun Zi specified *Xing* as the instinctive desire of humans: "Eyes like beautiful things, ears like wonderful sounds, the mouth likes delicious food, the heart likes profit, and the body likes comfort. These all come from mankind's instinctive desire," (*On the Evil of Human Nature*). What did Xun Zi's doctrine of the evil of human nature mean? Xun Zi stated,

*Xun Zi* (Part), annotated by Yang Jing, printed in Song Dynasty. *Xun Zi* was a Confucian classic. The edition that was annotated by Yang Jing during the Tang Dynasty is the earliest and most complete version.

People are born evil. Their kindness occurs after birth. Human beings like profit when they are born. Therefore, they vie for wealth and lose modesty. People loathe others when they are born. Therefore, they kill each other and lose honesty. Human beings like music and beauty when they are born. Therefore, they become lewd and lose rite. If human beings indulge themselves in their desires, they will plunder others and disturb the ritual order, which will result in riot. (*On the Evil of Human Nature*)

To Xun Zi, if people indulged themselves and followed their desires, there would be robbery, killing and lewdness (qualities that embodied the evil of human nature).

It is good to discuss *Wei* in relationship to *Xing* and the evil of human nature. Firstly, *Wei* differed from *Xing*: "Wei means the norms for the action and words one forms after long-time practice," (*Rectifying Names*). *Wei* was therefore thought of as something that could be gained as the result of long-standing practice and as something that could correct the evil of human nature:

> **People are born with desire. When their desires are not satisfied, people will pursue more. When their pursuits are not restrained, they will plunder. When people plunder, there will be disturbances. When disturbances comes, there will be poverty. The late king disliked disturbance and made rites to divide people's desires and to gratify their desires and pursuits. Then, people's desires will not exhaust their materials and their materials will not succumb to desire. To balance desires and materials, this is why rite has been made. (*On Rites*)**

Xun Zi elaborated on the difference between *Xing* and *Wei*:

> ***Xing* is what human beings are born with. It cannot be obtained through learning and efforts. Rite is what a sage makes. It can be obtained through learning and efforts. *Xing* is what people cannot obtain with learning and efforts. *Wei* is what people can obtain with learning and efforts. This is the difference between them. (*On the Evil of Human Nature*)**

> ***Xing* is like the raw wood; *Wei* is like the grand rite. (*On Rites*)**

Xun Zi defined the change from *Xing* to *Wei* as *Hua Xing Qi Wei* (*On the Evil of Human Nature*, to guide and reform human nature with propriety and law): "Therefore, the ruler should edify citizens with propriety and law so that they understand the need to be respectful and modest. Then, the citizens behave well and the country enjoys peace," (*On the Evil of Human Nature*).

As mentioned above, Xun Zi thought that kindness or morality was obtained after birth, and that human nature could be cultivated so that it became good (in spite of the fact that he thought that people were born evil).

In this sense, Xun Zi shared a similar view to Mencius who claimed, "All can become a sage like Yao and Shun." Xun Zi said,

**A man on the road can become a sage like Yu. Why? Yu became a sage as he practiced benevolence and righteousness. One can understand why he should do so. An ordinary man possesses the quality and possibility to know benevolence and righteousness; therefore, it is obvious that he can become a sage like Yu."** (*On the Evil of Human Nature*)

In other words, all might become a sage via *Hua Xing Qi Wei* (*On the Evil of Human Nature*, to guide and reform human nature with propriety and law). This idea was embodied in the view "A man on the road can become a sage like Yu."

In general, Xun Zi's doctrine on the evil of human nature was more profound than both Gao Zi's view that human nature was neutral and Mencius' doctrine on the goodness of human nature. Xun Zi did not just understand human nature in terms of natural attributes like Gao Zi nor did he just identify human nature with morality like Mencius. He discussed human nature in the context of social norms, which enabled him to understand the essence of human nature. However, Xun Zi's doctrine was not perfect. For instance, In *Xun Zi*, a man asked, "If people are born evil, are rite and righteousness evil when they come into being?" Xun Zi replied, "Rite and righteousness come from sages," (*On the Evil of Human Nature*). This, however, raises the question: "Where does the sage's kindness from?" Evidently, Xun Zi could not answer due to social constraints of his time. It is of note that Confucianism later accepted the doctrine of Mencius rather than that of Xun Zi, which sheds light of the thinking and moral judgment of the ancient Chinese.

## The Development of Theories on Human Nature

From the time of the Han Dynasty, the development of theories about human nature took place in two stages: during the Han and Tang dynasties and during the Song and Ming dynasties. During both of these stages the thoughts of Mencius and Xun Zi were absorbed and integrated into a common philosophical system.

In the Han and Tang dynasties, the typical way of thinking about human nature was the "Three-Grade Theory." Proposed by Dong Zhongshu, this theory divided man into three grades: high, middle, and low. These corresponded to sage, ordinary man and petty man respectively. Dong Zhongshu said that: "The nature of neither a sage nor a petty man can be changed. Only that of an ordinary man is changeable," (*Luxuriant Dew of the Spring and Autumn Annals* [*Chun Qiu Fan Lu*], *Shi Xing*). Evidently, Dong Zhongshu's view was influenced by Confucius who also believed that only wise and stupid men could not be transformed. To Dong Zhongshu, human nature therefore mainly referred to the nature of the ordinary man, which was reformable: "The nature of the ordinary man is like a silkworm cocoon or a bird's egg. A bird's egg turns to a young bird after 20 days. A silkworm cocoon turns to silk when its filaments have been heated in hot water. Human nature will be improved after edification," (*Shi Xing*). Meanwhile, Dong Zhongshu took the Yin-Yang Theory (a basic theory during the Han Dynasty) as his theoretical framework and observed that human nature also consisted of Yin and Yang. He said, "In the heaven, there are Yin and Yang, which are embodied by the greed and benevolence of humans," (*Shen Cha Ming Hao*). In this context Yang meant benevolence and goodness and Yin meant greed and evil. For Dong Zhonshu people were born with goodness and evil. Since there was both goodness and evil in the nature of the ordinary man, he thought that edification could and should play a crucial role in such a person's life. It is notable that Dong Zhongshu's theory combined the doctrines of Mencius and Xun Zi. It is also notable that it highlighted the importance of cultivation and edification (factors that both Mencius and Xun Zi had stressed). In this sense, he helped to bring the Confucian theory on human nature to a mature level. In the Tang Dynasty (618-907), Han Yu's theory on human nature basically inherited that of Dong Zhongshu.

It must be noted that Buddhist view on Buddha-nature (*Buddha-dhatu*) also concerned human

Dong Zhongshu (176-104 BC) was born in Guangchuan (today the northeast of Zaoqiang, Hebei Province). He was a philosopher and scholar on Confucian classics during the Western Han Dynasty. His views of "rejecting the other schools of thought and respecting only Confucianism" and "using morality first and punishment second" were accepted by Emperor Wu of the Han Dynasty. As a result, Confucianism became the social foundation of Chinese culture and influenced China for over 2,000 years.

nature and resembled Mencius' doctrine. Mencius concentrated on goodness while Buddhists focused on Buddha-nature. For instance, Zhu Dao sheng, who was a Buddhist scholar during the Eastern Jin Dynasty (317-420), thought that all living creatures had Buddha-nature. He said, "All living creatures should be considered as Buddha," and "All living creatures are Buddha." (*Commentaries on Lotus Sutra*). Hui Neng, an eminent monk, said, "One who understands Zen will consider all to be Buddha; one who does not will consider Buddha to be all," (*Platform Sutra* [*Tan Jing*], *Fu Zhu Pin*) and "One should seek Buddha nature in himself rather than the outer world," (*Yi Wen Pin*). Hui Neng's thought was also embodied in his reply to Shen Xiu: "Bodhi is fundamentally without any tree, /The bright mirror is also not a stand. /Fundamentally there is not a single thing, /Where could any dust be attracted?"

In the Song and Ming dynasties, the typical way of thinking about human nature was encapsulated in the theory of the "Duality of Human Nature," which was postulated by Zhang Zai and Zhu Xi. Zhang Zai called human nature the "Nature of the Heaven and Earth" and the "Nature of Temperature" and Zhu Xi called human nature the "Nature of Heaven's

Order" and the "Nature of Temperature." For instance, Zhu Xi said, "the Nature of the Heaven and Earth referred to *Li* (reason); the Nature of Temperature referred to *Li* (reason) and *Qi*," (*Words of Zhu Zi*, Vol. 1). [Note: *Qi* was a very complicated idea in Chinese philosophy. It was widely used and is hard to describe in English.] The "Duality of Human Nature Theory" was based on the idea that the world consisted of two parts: 1) "being" or "essence," and 2) "phenomenon" or "existence." Being or essence corresponded to the "Nature of the Heaven and Earth" or the "Nature of Heaven's Order," which was also known as "Natural Instinct". This was the most basic part of human nature, which was common to all. Phenomenon or existence corresponded to the other side of human nature that corresponded to the "Nature of Temperature," and consisted of Yin and Yang. This meant that human nature was both good and evil and that evil or badness came from the "Nature of Temperature." Zhang Zai's "Duality of Human Nature" theory differed from that of Zhu Xi. To Zhang Zai, the "Nature of the Heaven and Earth" came from *Qi* and accorded with the ontology of *Qi*. However, to Zhu Xi, the "Nature of Heaven's Order" came from *Li* (Reason) and accorded with the ontology of *Li* (Reason). However, Zhang Zai and Zhu Xi shared the same views on edification. They both observed that the "Nature of Temperature" should be reformed. For instance, Zhang Zai said, "One can transform his temperament through learning," (*Demystification of Confucianist Classics* [*Jing Xue Li Ku*], *Temperament*). This meant that the "Nature of Temperature" could turn to the "Nature of the Heaven and Earth." It can be seen that Zhang Zai's theory combined the doctrines of Mencius and Xun Zi, and that Zhang Zai's theory encapsulated more of Mencius' doctrine.

While it was true that the theory on human nature formulated by Chinese philosophers in the time between the Han and Tang dynasties and the Song and Ming dynasties became more systematized than it had been in Pre-Qin times, this did not mean that it was more profound. As a matter of fact, neither the "Three Grade Theory" nor the "Duality of Human Nature Theory" was as profound as the doctrines of Mencius and Xun Zi. This is because Mencius and Xun Zi considered the issue freely and managed to approach its essence, while philosophers in the time after the Qin and Han dynasties where more intent on pursuing the completeness of their theories and on meeting the needs of their imperial rulers.

It should also be noted that human nature related to edification. This link was widely acknowledged by Confucians and constituted the main direction and aim of their theories.

# The Taoist Outlook on Life

Taoists had a rich and distinct outlook on life although they seldom mentioned the ideal character. Both Lao Tzu and Chuang Tzu disbelieved in the existence of civilisation and this denial was embodied in their outlooks on life. Of the two, Lao Tzu was more experienced and sophisticated while Chuang Tzu was simpler and freer. This was because Lao Tzu lived a secular life but Chuang Tzu lived a monastic life.

## Lao Tzu's Outlook on Life

Lao Tzu's outlook on life accorded with his outlook on social issues and reflected his dialectical outlook. From Lao Tzu's outlook on life, we can discern his rich experience. For instance, Lao Tzu said, "Man can make himself safe if he compromises; branch can make itself straight if it bends. Emptiness will turn to fullness; oldness will turn to newness. Man can obtain more if he hopes less; man can delude himself if he hopes more," (*Lao Tzu*, Chapter 22). Here, Lao Tzu was expressing the view that a person could make himself more secure if he compromised. This shows that Lao Tzu had a profound experience and understanding of life. He also said, "One who knows his strength corrects his weaknesses and remains low like a gully… One who knows brightness keeps alert against darkness and views it as the rule… One who knows honor avoids shame and remains modest like a valley," (Chapter 28). Lao Tzu's dialectical outlook is shown in his thoughts on the relationship between goodness and evil, and upper and lower, as well as his thoughts on how to live with wisdom. Lao Tzu's thought was also embodied in other remarks, such as:

**The clear road seems obscure; the road that leads to the front seems to lead to the back; the smooth road seems rough. The lofty seems low; the honest seems dishonest; the sufficient seems**

Statue of Lao Tzu, at Qing-
yuan Mountain, in Quanzhou,
Fujian Province.

deficient; the strong seems weak; the simple seems cunning; the most rectangular seems edgeless. The great mind matures slowly; the large bell sounds silent; the obvious image seems invisible. (*Lao Tzu*, Chapter 41)

The perfect seems flawed but cannot be exhausted; the fullest seems empty but cannot be used up; the straightest seems curved; the smartest seems clumsy; the most eloquent seems taciturn. (Chapter 45)

Meanwhile, Lao Tzu advised that people should keep at an arm's length from fame, profit, wealth and achievement. He said,

One who pursues perfectness cannot achieve; one who displays his ability publicly cannot secure himself for long; one who owns wealth cannot maintain it. One who is rich and luxurious

will cause disaster to himself. One who has attained achievement should not claim credit. This is the *Tao*. (Chapter 9)

One who overvalues will pay more; one who owns excessively will lose more. One who is content with his lot will not be shamed and one who is conscious of his limit will not be endangered. This can secure him long life. (Chapter 44)

One must not be overbearing: "One who obtains success should not brag about it, nor show off, nor display self-conceit. He should ascribe his success to objective conditions rather than flaunt his superiority." (Chapter 30)

One must be careful and vigilant: "One often fails in a great undertaking when on the verge of success. One will not fail if he always keeps cautious." (Chapter 64)

In Lao Tzu's view, the best stance for a man to take was to show an impression of weakness: "One who is obstinate and strong will suffer catastrophe while one who is gentle and weak will enjoy peace… One who seems strong is in unfavorable position while one who seems weak is in favorable position," (Chapter 76) and "The law of a sage is to do but not to vie," (Chapter 81).

*Laojun*, painted in the 16th century. *Laojun* was the honorific name of Lao Tzu who was deified. Lao Tzu was the author of *Tao Te Ching* or *Lao Tzu*, the most important Taoist classic. He was born in the 6th century BC. It was said that when he was born, he was white-headed and spoke eloquently.

Lao Tzu views indicated his tact, flexibility, wisdom and even his trickery. In some sense, Lao Tzu's outlook on life summarized his experiences in life – it was a passive and somewhat dark view of society but one that was illuminating and useful for individuals who lived in a society where law was absent and despotism was rampant.

## Chuang Tzu's Outlook on Life

Chuang Tzu's outlook on life differed from that of Lao Tzu. Lao Tzu thought that one should live in the secular world and his outlook embodied the "art of living". In contrast, Chuang Tzu saw the cruelty in life and thought that one should live in the monastic world; therefore, his outlook on life presents us with a philosophical attitude or stance towards life.

Chuang Tzu's outlook on life was represented by the story of the Happy Excursion (*Xiao Yao You*) which meant "individual freedom". To Chuang Tzu, men were commonly not free as they were limited by various conditions ("You Dai" or "You Suo Dai" in Chuang Tzu's term). In "A Happy Excursion," Chuang Tzu recounted the story of an enormous legendary bird called Peng that flew over the wind. To the ordinary man, the bird Peng seemed free as "when it flies southwards, the water is smitten for a space of three thousand *Li* around while the bird itself mounts upon a great wind to a height of ninety thousand *Li*, for a flight of six months' duration." However, Chuang Tzu thought that the bird Peng was not free as it depended on the wind to fly. In other words, it would only know real freedom if it did not have to rely on any conditions, or if it could cast off any limits. In Chuang Tzu's view, the perfect, divine and virtuous man was one who had real freedom and relied on nothing. He said, "The perfect man ignores himself; the divine man ignores achievement; the true Sage ignores reputation." In some cases, Chuang Tzu called such men *Zhen Ren*: "A Zhen Ren in the past is neither pleased by life nor saddened by death. He does not rejoice at a birth or dread death. He leaves and comes freely," (*The Great and Most Honored Master*). Here, Chuang Tzu is expressing the attitude of a Zhen Ren towards life and death: to accept life and death calmly and let them happen naturally. In fact, for Chuang Tzu the most critical quality of the perfect, divine and virtuous man (or the Zhen Ren) was that they could transcend all troubles and puzzles, such as

Portrait of Chuang Tzu. Chuang Tzu (369-286 BC), a philosopher, also known as Chuang Zhou, was born in Meng (today Mengcheng, Anhui Province).

life and death, age and youth, gain and loss, and praise and criticism, and so finally reach the highest level of life.

Chuang Tzu's ideas sound impossible as humans cannot act without limits and must rely on society and nature. Therefore, absolute freedom cannot really exist. Nevertheless, Chuang Tzu's outlook on life was significant. He did not pursue wealth, profit and fame and led a poor life. His outlook on life was clearly indicated in a story in *Qiu Shui*:

**Chuang Tzu was fishing at Puhe River. The King of the Kingdom Chu assigned two officials to address him and say, "The king wants to entrust his affairs to you." Chuang Tzu held his fishing rod and turned his back on them. He said, "I heard there was a divine turtle in Kingdom Chu that died 2,000 years ago. The king enveloped it with brocade and placed it in an ancestral temple. Did the turtle choose to leave the bone valued by human or to live in the mud freely?" The two officials answered, "To live in the mud freely." Chuang Tzu said, "Please go back. I would like to 'live in the mud freely.'"[33]**

In addition, Chuang Tzu was happy with his destitute life: "I rove freely, not knowing what I pursue. I stroll leisurely, not knowing where I go. However, the numerous visitors are seeing the secular world," (*Freedom and Tolerance*). Chuang Tzu presented an image of life in which a man could rove in amongst nature, desiring for nothing, strolling at his leisure, with no idea of his destination, and appreciating the beauty of the world and of real life. It is notable that Chuang Tzu's heart was imbued with a pleasure that could not be described or expressed with words.

In summary, Chuang Tzu's outlook on life embodied his indifference to fame and profit, his optimism, his dissatisfaction with reality, and his fondness for seclusion, in short, his desire and pursuit of freedom[34]. Undoubtedly, Chuang Tzu's outlook on life played a positive role in Chinese history and brought a breath of fresh air to Chinese society. In fact, Chuang Tzu's outlook on life exerted a profound influence on the intellectuals who came after him and became one of the best and most valued qualities of the Chinese.

33. In *Qiu Shui*, it was recorded: "Hui Shi was prime minister of the Kingdom of Liang. Zhuang Zi visited him. A man told Hui Shi, 'Zhuang Zi comes here to replace you to be prime minster.' Hui Shi feared this and ordered men to seek Zhuang Zi for three days. Zhuang Zi saw Hui Shi and said, 'In the south, there was a bird called Yuan Chu. Do you hear that? Yuan Chu was flying towards the North Sea from the South Sea. It never rested unless the tree it rested in was a phoenix tree, never ate unless the fruit it ate was bamboo, and never drank unless the water it drank was sweet. Meanwhile, an owl got a rotten mouse. When Yuan Chu flew by the mouse, the owl raised head and uttered fearful sound. Now, are you frightening me with Kingdom Liang?'"

34. A similar thought can be seen in the ideal Confucian character. However, the ideal Confucian character was focused on the secular life or society, especially the ideal that one should possess the sage's virtue and practice the ruler's policy, so Confucianism could not avoid the pursuit of and reliance on fame.

# WHAT IS THE STRUCTURE OF KNOWLEDGE?

In addition to considering the outer world and reality, ancient Chinese philosophers also dealt with the inner world of human thought. In fact, knowledge played a vital role in their discussions on the nature of the world, the relationship between things, human nature, and the ideal character. Therefore, knowledge was thought of as the way by which people obtained truth or Tao. This raised the question, how did people understand the world and themselves? Chinese philosophers discussed many issues on this topic, such as the ability of knowledge, the relationship between knowledge and the object, the structure of knowledge, the form or stage of knowledge and the relationship between knowledge and action. Thinking on these issues constituted a prominent feature of Chinese philosophy. We should note three key points relating to philosophical thoughts about knowledge. First, thoughts on knowledge began to appear in Pre-Qin times and developed over a long period of history. Second, such thoughts concerned the relationship between the subject and object and the conflict between materialism and thought, which happened similarly in the history of Western philosophy. Third, for Confucianism, knowledge, or "investigating things and gaining knowledge," marked the beginning of the process that would allow one to possess the sage's virtue and practice the ruler's policy.

# The Source and Ability of Knowledge

The "source" and "ability" of knowledge were two basic or primary issues or questions that ancient Chinese philosophers considered in connection with the concept of knowledge. The question of the source of knowledge looked at how knowledge was formed and discussed the essence of thinking and existence. The question of the ability of knowledge looked at the unity of thinking and existence. Ancient Chinese philosophy provided answers to these questions and presented these in the form of various concepts or ideas, such as "Knowing and not Knowing," "Mind and Object," "Name and Substance" and "Language and Meaning."

## Knowing and Not Knowing

Knowing (meaning knowledge and understanding) was an important part of the ancient Chinese philosophy on knowledge. Discussions on this topic, covered questions such as: Could people acquire knowledge? Could people understand the world? There were a number of different opinions on these issues.

Knowing (*Zhi*) appeared as a concept very early on in Chinese history. In *Zuo Zhuan*, the word "knowing" was widely used and, in the late Spring and Autumn Period, a basic understanding of knowing was developed. Confucius was the first to discuss the idea of knowing in a profound way. For instance, Confucius warned his disciples: "If you know, recognize that you know; if you don't know, then realize that you don't know. This is knowledge," (*The Analects, Wei Zheng*). Here, Confucius was clearly differentiating "knowing" from "not knowing." Confucius also explained how he had made progress in learning: "When I was 15, I determined to learn; in my thirties, I was independent; in my forties, I was free of temptation; in my fifties, I knew fate; in my sixties, I was satisfied with everything; in my seventies, I do whatever I want to do," (*The Analects, Wei Zheng*).

Obviously, Confucius took a positive attitude towards knowledge. Subsequently, many schools of thoughts in Pre-Qin times expressed their views on knowledge and the idea of knowing:

> Mohism said, "Knowing means a person's ability in knowledge." (*The Book of Mozi, Canon I*)
>
> Xun Zi said, "What makes a person pursue knowledge is their nature and what can be understood is the law of things." (*Xun Zi, Removing Obstructions*)
>
> Han Fei said, "Ears and eyes are what one is born with; action and consideration are what one does after birth." (*Han Fei Zi, Explaining Lao Tzu*)

Statue of Mo Zi. Mo Zi was also called Mo Di and was born in present-day Tengzhou, Shandong Province. He was a famous philosopher, scientist, human rights activist, and military strategist who lived during the Warring States Period. He proposed the ideas of "Universal Love" and " No Invasion" and founded Moism. He was the author of *Mo Zi*.

Obviously, their views had a strong Gnostic character.

Taoists had a unique view on knowledge. Lao Tzu expressed his deep understanding of knowledge: "One will succeed if he acts after he knows the rules; one will meet obstacles if he acts before he knows the rules," (*Lao Tzu*, Chapter 16). Lao Tzu clearly stated the importance of knowing the rules. Unlike Confucius, Lao Tzu stressed that "One cannot bear in mind authority and subjectivity" and that "One can secure himself when he does not obtain knowledge," (Chapter 19). Certainly, Lao Tzu's view was based on the practical need to rule a country rather than on an epistemologist stance. Chuang Tzu largely inherited Lao Tzu's view. Chuang Tzu noted that human knowledge did not cover everything in the universe. He said that: "People in the past had limited knowledge," and "One who knows that there are some

things he does not know has reached the highest level," (*Chuang Tzu, On the Similarity between Things*). Chuang Tzu's view sounded reasonable. However, he fell into the trap of agnosticism:

**Let me ask you. How do you know what I say I know means I do not know? How do you know what I say I do not know means I know?' (*On the Similarity Between Things*)**

**One did not realize the dream when he was dreaming, or deciphered another dream in the present dream. He realized the dream only after he woke up. The great realization comes after a great dream. The stupid man knows he had a dream, but he is still in the dream. (*On the Similarity between Things*)**

Chuang Tzu drew the conclusion that: "Human's life is limited while knowledge is unlimited. A man will exhaust himself if he pursues knowledge with his limited life," (*On Health*).

In addition, for Chinese philosophers, knowledge or understanding related to the testing of knowledge or understanding. For instance, Xun Zi said, "One view can be argued and tested," (*Xun Zi, On the Evil of Human Nature*). Han Fei said, "To justify one's view, we should see whether it accords with reality; to justify one's words, we should test them with practice," (*Han Fei Zi, Killing the Treacherous Court Official*). Wang Chong said, "One cannot convince another if he lists facts without evidence, no matter how persuasive his views sound," (*Critical Essays, On Knowledge and Practice*). Their thoughts all highlighted the importance of testing knowledge. They also underlined the need for there to be consistency between knowledge and facts.

## Mind and Object

The concept of "mind and object" related to such questions as: "Where did knowledge originate?" "How did knowledge come into being?" "Did knowledge originate from objects or the mind?" Chinese philosophers came up with a number of different answers to these questions –

these embodied the difference between materialism and mentalism.

It was Confucius who first discussed these issues. He said, "He who knew knowledge when he was born was the most talented and he who obtained knowledge through learning was the second," (*The Analects, Ji Shi*). Here, Confucius was indicating two ways to obtain knowledge: being born with knowledge (congenital) and obtaining knowledge through learning (postnatal). Although Confucius' dualism may seem vague and ambivalent, it played an important role in Chinese philosophy and established the foundations for materialism and mentalism. Confucius himself did not consider that he had been born with knowledge, "I did not know knowledge when I was born. I liked ancient culture and studied hard," (*Shu Er*).

In Pre-Qin times, most scholars took a materialist stance and ascribed to the "Theory of Reflection" with respect to the origin of knowledge. In other words, they thought that knowledge came from people's contact with nature. Mo Zi said, "If one saw a ghost, he must think that there was a ghost in the world, and vice versa," (*Mo Zi, On Ghost and God II*). Mo Zi took the idea of "seeing for oneself" as the foundation of knowledge, an approach which was accepted by Mohism. In *The Book of Mo Zi*, it was stated, "Knowledge is what one contacts," (*Canon I*) and "Knowledge means that one can describe what one sees vividly," (*Explanations to The Book of Mo Zi I*). Xun Zi said, "Knowledge means wisdom when it stands up to a test," (*Xun Zi, Rectifying Names*). These views indicted the importance of contact between subject and object. Han Fei expressed a similar view in his critique of apriorism: "Foreknowledge relates to the rule that one expresses before things have displayed. Foreknowledge is conjecture without ground,"[35] (*Han Fei Zi, Explaining Lao Tzu*).

Mencius' theory on knowledge inherited Confucius' concept that someone could be "born with knowledge" and had a mentalist character. Mencius said, "Good quality is what a person possesses without learning; good knowledge is what a person obtains without thinking," (*Mencius, With All Heart I*). On morality, Mencius said, "Benevolence, righteousness, rite, and wisdom are not given by others but are inherent in a person," (*Gao Zi I*). In relation to the apriorist stance, Mencius said,

---

35. In the history of Western philosophy, empiricists like Bacon and Locke held similar views to Han Fei.

"One will know his nature if he fully explores his mind. One will know Tao if he knows his nature," (*With All Heart I*) and "The cardinal rule for learning is nothing but to discover one's nature," (*Gao Zi I*). Mencius also agreed with the idea of foreknowledge and admitted that he had foreknowledge via Yi Yin's words: "(Yi Yin said) the heaven creates people to allow those with insight to enlighten those without it. I am one of those with insight and I will enlighten them. Nobody can achieve it, but I," (*Wan Zhang I*).

It is noticeable that the mind-object issue was dealt with as a form-spirit (*Shen*) issue. In this context *Shen* referred to ghost as in spirit, not as in ghost-God. This issue was mentioned in Pre-Qin times. For example, Xun Zi revealed that form appeared earlier than spirit: "Spirit will appear when form has been complete," (*Xun Zi, Treatise on Heaven*). It was also discussed in medical theory. In *The Inner Canon of the Yellow Emperor*, it was said, "The five organs in *Zang* accumulate vitality, blood and spirit," (*Central Area, On Meridian System and Blood*). In *Huai Nan Zi*, it was postulated that spirit should determine form: "It is favorable if spirit decides form while harmful if form decides spirit," (*Treatise on Original Tao*). The Buddhist view was that spirit was immortal (which made the issue more complicated). Huan Tan, a philosopher from the late Western Han Dynasty and the early Eastern Han Dynasty, compared the spirit to a candle fire in order to refute the Buddhist view: "That the spirit relies on form resembles the fire of a candle," (*New Thoughts* [*Xin Lun*], *Ridding Obstructions*). Later, Hui Yuan, a Buddhist philosopher who lived during the Eastern Jin Dynasty, used fagot-fire as a metaphor to demonstrate the immortality of the spirit: "That the fire was transferred to a fagot resembles the transfer of the spirit to form. That the fire was transferred to different fagots resembles the transfer of the spirit to different forms," (*On Monks Should Not Respect the King*). During the Southern Dynasty (420-589), Fan Zhen fundamentally deconstructed the Buddhist view: "Spirit and form are inseparable. Spirit exists when form is present and disappears when form is absent," (*On the Non-Existence of Spirit*).

Buddhist theory also dealt with the mind-object issue. Indeed, this was the most basic question in Buddhist philosophy. The way Buddhists approached this issue had a strong mentalist character. For instance, Zhi Yi, a monk from the Tiantai Sect, held the view of "one idea and three thousand worlds":

*Three Laughing Men at Tiger Creek*, painted during the Song Dynasty and now part of the collection of the Taipei Palace Museum. It depicts an event from the Eastern Jin Dynasty when Tao Yuanming, a Confucian scholar, and Lu Xiujing, a Taoist, visited Hui Yuan, an eminent monk who practiced Buddhism at Lushan Mountain. In their return, they laughed and walked. Hui Yuan sent them off and stepped into Tiger Creek that was as turbulent as tiger's roar. The three men saw each other and laughed.

**One idea represents ten Dharma realms. One Dharma realm extends to ten and one hundred Dharma realms. One Dharma realm includes thirty worlds, and one hundred Dharma realms include three thousand worlds, which all exist in one idea. (*The Analects of Monk Zhi Yi* [*Mo He Zhi Guan*], Vol. 5)**

Xuan Zang, a monk from the Weishi Sect, thought that everything could be transformed through the mind: "Therefore, all that seems achievable or unachievable, virtual or realistic, originates from the mind," (*Discourse on the Perfection of Consciousness-Only* [*Cheng Wei Shi Lun*], Vol. 7). Zong Mi, a monk from the Huayan Sect said, "In the real Dharma realm, all can be reduced to the mind,"

*The Sixth Patriarch Hui Neng*, painted by Ding Guanpeng during the Qing Dynasty. Hui Neng (638-713) was viewed as the sixth Patriarch in Chinese Zen. He was a famous Buddhist reformer and one of the great philosophers of Chinese history. He introduced Indian Buddhism to China, sinicized it and founded Chinese Zen.

(*Notes on Gates in Huayan Dharma Realm*). Hui Neng, a Zen monk, took "non-mind" as his cardinal rule: "One who realizes non-mind will realize all and reach the highest level," (*Platform Sutra* [*Tan Jing*], *Bo Re Pin*). This meant that a man should keep his mind unaffected by external objects.

After the Song Dynasty, discussions about the mind-object issue returned to a Confucian stance. Ontologically, Zhang Zai and Zhu Xi took different opinions. Epistemologically, they were both influenced by Confucius' dualism. Zhang Zai observed that "Man obtains knowledge using his eyes and ears to perceive it. Man perceives the external objects with his mind." He also observed that "the knowledge that eyes and ears can perceive does not rely on experience," (*Correcting the Unenlightened, The Great Mind*). Similarly, Zhu Xi believed that, "One knows the truth by touching the object." He also believed that, "Knowledge exists in the mind of all," (*Commentaries to Selected Great Learning*). In contrast, Lu Jiuyuan and Wang Yangming inherited the thoughts of Mencius. Lu Jiuyuan said, "All can think and bear ideas in mind, so what one thinks is truth," ("To Li Zai"). Wang Yangming said, "What one thinks is truth. In spite of the fact that the objects are different, they all express one's idea," (*The Analects of Wang Yangming* [*Chuan Xi Lu*], Vol. 1). Wang Yangming's view was fully embodied in the following quotation:

When you do not see the flower, it remains invisible as your mind has not perceived it. When you see the flower, it presents the diverse colors to you. Thus, the flower does not exist out of your mind. (*The Analects of Wang Yangming* [*Chuan Xi Lu*], Vol. 3)

My mind dominates the heaven, the earth, ghosts, and God. Without my mind, how could the heaven be worshipped? How could the earth be respected? How could disaster and fortune be discerned by ghosts and God? (*The Analects of Wang Yangming* [*Chuan Xi Lu*], Vol. 3)

Here, it is clear that Wang Yangming's views had developed into solipsism[36] (the belief that one can only be certain that one's mind exists). Obviously, his views were therefore criticized by materialist philosophers. For instance, Wang Tingxiang said, "A sage cannot know the truth if he does not see and perceive the object," (*Ya Shu*, Vol. 1). Wang Fuzhi said, "One perceives the object and then forms ideas in the mind. Therefore, one cannot form ideas if he has not perceived the object," (*Notes on Correcting the Unenlightened*, Note on Hexagram Qian II). It is notable that Wang Fuzhi revised the Buddhist concepts of *Neng* (Subject)-*Suo* (Object) to explain the mind-object relationship:

*Suo* (Object) means one thing that can be used. *Neng* (Subject) means the function one thing serves. This is the difference between *Suo* and *Neng*. It was reasonable that Buddhists used them in dualism. *Suo* must depend on form and *Neng* must depend on function. *Suo* can be used through *Neng* and *Neng* can function through *Suo*. (*Elaborations on the Book of Documents, Duke Zhao's Memorial to the King and No Comfort*)

Here, *Neng* was the subject and *Suo* was the object. Wang Fuzhi thought that it was sensible for Buddhists to use the two terms to differentiate the mind from objects, but he also thought that

---

36. It was similar to George Berkeley's thought that objects existed as they could be perceived.

they overstated the importance of the mind and devalued objects, (*Elaborations on the Book of Documents, Duke Zhao's Memorial to the King and No Comfort*). However, Wang Fuzhi used Neng-Suo and Form-Function to explain the mind-object relationship. This highlighted the importance of reflection and the spirit of initiative, and criticized the wrong understanding of knowledge.

## Name and Substance

In ancient Chinese philosophy, the name-substance issue was closely related to knowledge. Specifically, there were two main schools of thought: One believed that name decided substance and the other believed that substance decided name.

Confucius was the main representative of the first school of thought. His core idea was to "correct name" first:

**If terminology is not corrected, then what is said cannot be followed. If what is said cannot be followed, then work cannot be accomplished. If work cannot be accomplished, then ritual and music cannot be developed. If ritual and music cannot be developed, then criminal punishments will not be appropriate. If criminal punishments are not appropriate, the people cannot make a move. (*The Analects, Zi Lu*)**

It must be noted that by "correcting name," Confucius meant the restoration of the hierarchy system of the Zhou Dynasty. In other words, the establishment of present order (Substance) with past rite (Name).

Confucius' thought was inherited by Dong Zhongshu. Dong Zhongshu said, "Therefore, all things are defined according to their names which are given by the heaven," (*Luxuriant Dew of the Spring and Autumn Annals* [*Chun Qiu Fan Lu*], *Shen Cha Ming Hao*) and "To decide the curve or straight, one must use a line marker. To judge right or wrong, one must use the criterion of the sage," (*Luxuriant Dew of the Spring and Autumn Annals* [*Chun Qiu Fan Lu*], *Shen Cha Ming Hao*). Name stood here for the criteria used to judge right and wrong.

These thoughts raise the question, "how was name formed?" Dong Zhongshu observed that names and ideas, or moral standards and political rules were made by sages: "Name is what the sage used to define things," (*Luxuriant Dew of the Spring and Autumn Annals* [*Chun Qiu Fan Lu*], *Shen Cha Ming Hao*). In fact, Dong Zhongshu expressed the view that history was created by sages. He also believed that sages established names to convey the heaven's will: "The correct names come from the heaven that gives names to display its will," (*Luxuriant Dew of the Spring and Autumn Annals* [*Chun Qiu Fan Lu*], *Shen Cha Ming Hao*). This belief endowed the concept of "name" with a mysterious character.

Mo Zi was the representative of the second school of thought relating to the name-substance issue. In *Mo Zi*, it was recorded:

**A blind man said, "*Ai* means white and *Qian* means black. Those who can see cannot change them." Then, people combine white with black and let him tell. The blind man**

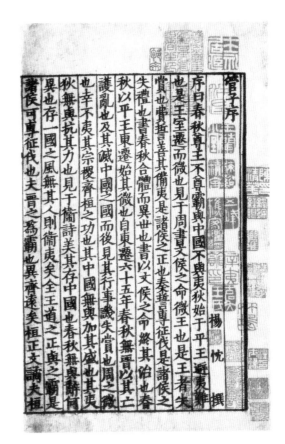

Preface to *Guan Zi*, written by Yang Chen during the Song Dynasty. Guan Zhong (?-645 BC) also known as Guan Yiwu and Guan Zizhong, was born in Yishang (in today's Anhui Province). He was a politician of the Kingdom of Qi during the Spring and Autumn Period. As a collection of the views of schools during the Warring States Period, *Guan Zi* was compiled by the Guanzhong School rather than Guan Zhong. It consisted of 24 volumes and 8 categories, and included the views of Legalism, Confucianism, Taoism, Yin-Yang School, School of Names, School of the Military and Agriculturalism.

cannot distinguish. I said, "The blind man cannot tell the white and black, as he distinguishes them based on the name rather than substance. (*On Valuing Righteousness*)

Here, Mo Zi puts forward a simple materialism which was later taken forward by his followers. For instance:

Name is what is used to describe. Substance is what name describes. Name and substance are consistent with each other. (Explanation to *The Book of Mo Zi I*)

There is substance first and then the name of it. There is no name if no substance. (Explanation to *The Book of Mo Zi II*)

In *The Canon of Mo Zi*, this idea was summarized as "illustrating substance with name," ("Xiao Qu"). It was a view that was held by many philosophers. Guan Zi said, "To testify the substance with name and to establish the name with substance," (*Guan Zi, The Nine Rules*). Xun Zi said, "Name is made to denote substance," (*Xun Zi, Rectifying Names*). These philosophers all expressed a similar view: that a name or idea represented reality and accorded with reality[37].

It should be noted that the name-substance issue also concerned logic. For instance, Gongsun Long said, "Name represents the nature of substance. If the name does not denote the substance, we

---

37. In Western philosophy, the name-substance issue was similarly discussed. In Scholasticism, there were realism and nominalism. According to Thilly, the issue played an important role in Greek philosophical theory, and was discussed by Plato and Aristotle. In Scholasticism, some agreed with Platonic realism and thought that "idea" appeared earlier than substance, some agreed with Aristotelian realism and thought that "idea" existed in objects, and some agreed with nominalism and thought that "idea" was the name of objects and that it appeared later than substance (neither earlier than nor in substance). See Thilly, *A History of Western Philosophy*. Beijing: Commercial Press. 1999, p. 183. Of course, name and substance meant different things in Chinese and Western philosophies.

cannot define the substance with the name; if the substance does not exist in the name, we cannot illustrate the name with the substance," (*Book of Gongsun Long, On Name and Substance*). Xun Zi said, "Name the similar objects with similar names and different objects with different names. Use a single word or multiple words to name objects as long as they clearly denote objects. If not, it does not harm to use common names," (*Xun Zi, Rectifying Names*). These philosophers were dealing with the idea of categories, for example, giving similar names to similar objects and different names to different objects. In Mohism, this approach was reduced to "define and call with category," ("Xiao Qu"). Xun Zi stressed, "This is why one must confirm the name of a substance with a number and a key point for establishing the name," (*Xun Zi, Rectifying Names*).

## Language and Meaning

Chinese philosophers also considered the relationship between language and meaning and how this related to knowledge.

Lao Tzu was the first philosopher who discussed the relationship between language and meaning. For instance, he highlighted the ineffableness of *Tao*:

> **The Tao that can be trodden is not the enduring and unchanging Tao. The name that can be named is not the enduring and unchanging name. (*Lao Tzu*, Chapter 1)**

He also discussed the discordance between language and meaning, or the virtuality of language:

> **The smartest seems clumsy; the most eloquent seems taciturn. (Chapter 45)**
>
> **One who knows does not speak; one who speaks does not know. (Chapter 56)**
>
> **What sounds pleasant is unbelievable; what sounds unpleasant is believable. (Chapter 81)**

Confucius held similar views: "A gentleman should be cautious in speech and diligent in action," (*The Analects, Li Ren*). Here we notice how the ancient Chinese philosophers viewed language: Language was used to express thoughts and form should therefore not be overstated.

Chuang Tzu also considered the relationship between language and meaning. He also thought that language could not express the abstract Tao: "Tao cannot be heard. What can be heard is not Tao. Tao cannot be seen. What can be seen is not Tao. Tao cannot be spoken. What can be spoken is not Tao," (*Chuang Tzu, Knowledge Rambling in the North*). Fei Qi summarized Chuang Tzu's thoughts into three main ideas: That abstract language cannot express the concrete objects; that an unchangeable idea cannot express change; that a limited idea cannot express an unlimited meaning[38]. In addition, Chuang Tzu believed that language could not express a person's experience in mind. In *Chuang Tzu*, the following illustrative story was recorded:

**Lun Bian said, Wood is cut to make the wheel. If the wheel hole is wide, the wheel will loosen; if the wheel hole is narrow, the spoke will not enter. Only when the wheel hole is neither wide nor narrow will the wheel work well. I can understand but cannot express the rule. I cannot clearly tell it to my son, and my son cannot learn it from I.** (*The Heavenly Tao*)

In fact, he thought that it was common for someone to know something but not to be able to express it[39]. More importantly, Chuang Tzu was the first to discuss the nature of the language-meaning issue:

---

38. Feng Qi, *The Development of Logic in Ancient Chinese Philosophy*, Vol. 1. Shanghai: Shanghai People's Publishing House, 1983, pp. 210-212.

39. In the West, a similar thought was proposed by Polanyi in the 20th century. In "On Silence," the second part of *Personal Knowledge*, Polanyi stated, "To assert that I possess the knowledge I cannot express does not mean to deny I can tell it, but to deny that I can tell it properly." Michael Polanyi, *Personal Knowledge: Toward a Post-critical Philosophy*. Guiyang: Guizhou People's Publishing House, 2000, p. 135.

Fish tackle is used to catch fish. Man forgets it after he catches fish. A net is used to catch rabbits. Man forgets it after he catches a rabbit. Language is used to express thought. Man forgets it after he obtains the meaning. (*The External Objects*)

To Chuang Tzu, language was useless after it had expressed a thought. Later, in *Commentaries on Book of Change*, this thought was summarized as "Language and words cannot accurately express thought," (*Xi Ci I*).

In the Wei and Jin Dynasties, Wang Bi expressed new views based on Chuang Tzu and the *Commentaries on Book of Change*:

Phenomenon expresses the idea. Language expresses the phenomenon... Therefore, language clarifies phenomenon, and one forgets language after he understands the phenomenon; phenomenon indicates an idea, and one forgets phenomenon after he obtains the idea. This resembles that the net is on the rabbit, but the man has caught the rabbit and forgotten the net, and that the fish tackle is on the fish, but the man has caught the fish and forgotten the fish tackle... One forgets the phenomenon as he has obtained the idea; one forgets the language, as he has understood the phenomenon. One obtains the idea only when he has forgotten the idea and the phenomenon only when he has forgotten the phenomenon. (*Brief Interpretations of Book of Change, Elucidating the Image*)

Chuang Tzu thought that one should obtain an idea first before one forgets language, whereas Wang Bi thought that one should forget language first before one obtains an idea. Wang Bi subverted Chuang Tzu's view. Although there was an obvious mistake in his view, Wang Bi deconstructed the dependence on language. Later, Zeng Zhao descried *prajna* (*Bo Re*, wisdom) in a similar way: "The most profound wisdom cannot be clearly expressed through language and phenomenon," (*On the Unspeakableness of Prajna*). In short, ancient Chinese philosophers had a dialectical outlook on language and believed that language could express and restrict thought.

# The Structure or Form of Knowledge

Ancient Chinese philosophers thought deeply about how to obtain knowledge and the form of knowledge. They considered the following questions: What were the ways to obtain knowledge? What were the forms of knowledge? What roles did the different forms play?

## Information and Thinking

For Chinese philosophers, the information-thinking issue was a concept that was related to the mind-object issue. For them, thinking related to the source of knowledge while information related to the process of knowledge. Although the focus of these two issues was different, they shared some similarities. They were both forms and stages of knowledge, equivalent to what we now call perceptual knowledge and rational knowledge. Ancient Chinese philosophers considered these issues at a very early point in the country's history and their theories reached a high level of sophistication[40].

Confucius was the first philosopher who discussed information and thinking from the

---

40. In some sense, this was similar to the difference between empiricism and rationalism in Western modern philosophy. For instance, Thilly said, "Modern philosophy has been divided into rationalism and empiricism based on the source of knowledge, ration or experience." He also mentioned that: "Modern philosophy provided different answers to the source of knowledge." These included: (a) Real knowledge does not come from sensual perception or experience and has its basis in thought or rationality. This view embodied apriorism or rationalism. (b) There is no inherent truth. All knowledge comes from sensual perception or experience. This view embodied empiricism or sensualism. Thilly, *A History of Western Philosophy*. Beijing: Commercial Press, 1999, pp. 283-284.

perspective of learning and thinking. One well-known Confucian saying is particularly relevant: "Learning without thought is indiscriminate; thinking without learning is perilous," (*The Analects, Wei Zheng*)? Here, Confucius was stressing that one must combine learning and thinking, both of which must not be neglected. However, to Confucius, learning or seeing was more important:

> **Hear, and then choose the good to learn; see, and then remember in heart. (*Shu Er*)**

> **It is in vain I do not eat or sleep all day to think. It is better to learn. (*King Ling of Wei*)**

Lao Tzu held totally different views to Confucius:

> **One can know what happens in the world when he does not travel around; one can sense Tao when he does not see the window. (*Lao Tzu*, Chapter 47)**

> **One who learns progresses day by day while one who pursues Tao retrogresses day by day until the state of non-action has been achieved. (Chapter 48)**

Mohism valued the role that the senses played in knowledge as Mohists participated in practice and production. Mo Zi said, "To judge whether one object is

Wang Chong (27-about 97 AD), also known as Wang Zhongren, was born in Shangyu, Kuaiji (today in Zhejiang Province). He was a philosopher and literary theorist during the Easter Han Dynasty. *Critical Essays*, a representative work of Wang Chong, was a monumental atheist work in the history of Chinese philosophy.

Lu Jiuyuan (1139-1193), also known as Lu Zijing, Old Man at Xiangshan Mountain, and Mr. Xiangshan, was born in Jinyu, Fuzhou (today in Jiangxi Province). Although he and Zhu Xi were representatives of the School of Mind during the Southern Song Dynasty, they held contradictory views. He and Wang Shouren were called the School of Lu-Wang.

present or not, one must take what he sees and hears as the criterion," (*Mo Zi, On Ghost and God II*). Obviously, this view had a strong empirical character. However, this empiricist stance was changed in later Mohism, as shown in these statements: "That one can judge the object results from the observation of the mind," and "That one can obtain another's idea results from the analysis of the mind," (*The Book of Mo Zi, Canon I*).

Mencius highlighted the importance of mind or thinking. This certainly extended Mencius' mentalist view of the mind-object issue. Mencius said, "The eyes and ears cannot think, so they are deceived by the external object. One will be misled when he makes contact with the object. Mind can think. One can obtain ideas if the mind thinks and one cannot obtain ideas if one does not," (*Mencius, Gao Zi I*). In addition, Mencius called mind the "Great Form" (*Da Ti*) and sense the "Minor Form" (*Xiao Ti*): "If one firstly establishes the Great Form, the Minor Form will not be changed," (*Gao Zi I*). Mencius' understanding had a strong rationalist character.

In the late Warring States Period, Xun Zi considered the issue in a deeper way. Xun Zi called sense *Tian Guan* (sensual organs) and thinking *Tian Jun* (heart). He said, "The ear, eye, nose, mouth, and body cannot be replaced as they sense different objects. They are the sensual organs that humans are born with. The heart lies in the center and controls the five organs. It is the organ ruling the others," (*Treatise on Heaven*). This raises the question, what's the relationship between *Tian Guan* (sensual organs) and *Tian Jun* (heart)? Xun Zi explained, "The heart can testify what the organs sense. Nevertheless, that must depend on the ear that can hear and the eye that can see. Therefore, the role the heart plays must rely on the sensual organs that sense the objects." (*Rectifying Names*). In other words, he thought that the information one obtained from the sensual organs must be processed by thinking, which itself was based on the material the organs provided. Obviously, Xun Zi presented a more accurate understanding of the relationship between information and thinking than previous philosophers. Wang Chong held similar views to Xun Zi. Wang Chong attached great importance to sense and experience: "One must judge based on what one hears and sees," (*Critical Essays, On Knowledge and Practice*). In addition, Wang Chong valued the role of thinking: "When a man judges right or wrong according to what he sees and hears rather than what he thinks in his heart, he will believe in falsity and consider the right to be wrong. Therefore, a man must judge based on what he thinks in his heart," (*On Simple Funeral*).

In addition, in the important Confucian classic, the *Doctrine of the Mean*, there are some ideas that had a great impact on the Confucian theory on knowledge:

**A gentleman should study extensively, inquire prudently, think carefully, distinguish clearly, and practice earnestly.**

**A gentleman respects the nature given by the heaven and learns *Tao*, which extends his knowledge, acts in accordance with morality, and follows the *Doctrine of the Mean*.**

In the Song Dynasty, scholars attached more importance to thinking. For instance, Zhang Zai said, "One can hold the world when he extends the heart. Objects are immeasurable so the heart is limited. The heart of the ordinary man is limited by experience while that of a sage is not, as the sage considers all to be himself," (*Correcting the Unenlightened, The Great Mind*). Zhu Xi said, "The ear controls hearing and the eye controls seeing. They cannot think, so they are deceived by objects," and "The heart can think and controls thinking," (*Commentaries to Mencius, Selection of Gao Zi I*). In the School of Mind, the views of Lu Jiuyuan and Wang Yangming extended to the

mind-object issue:

> What matters in learning is that one must explore the truth with one's heart. (Lu Jiuyuan, "To Li Zai")

> Conscience exists even if it cannot be seen and heard, so it does not rely on seeing and hearing. (*The Analects of Wang Yangming* [*Chuan Xi Lu*], Vol. 3)

The views of these philosophers obviously focused on thinking.

Wang Fuzhi returned to the theories of Confucius and Xun Zi. On "investigating things and gaining knowledge," Wang Fuzhi said,

> Investigating things means to collect phenomena in the past and present and discover the truth. Gaining knowledge means to reveal the hidden ideas. Without the latter, the ideas in objects cannot be embodied; without the former, the truth will be led in the wrong direction. When investigating things and gaining knowledge is combined, one can succeed in learning. (*Elaborations on the Book of Documents, On the Effect of Fate II*)

Wang Fuzhi's views encompass the mutual reliance between sensibility and rationality. It also embodies the dialectic outlook[41].

---

41. Interestingly, Kant also reconciled rationalism and empiricism. Kant observed that the two theories sounded reasonable or advisable.

## Gradual Study and Epiphany

Gradual study and epiphany were important ideas in Buddhist philosophy and were related to the method and form of knowledge. Gradual study described the process in which a person realized the truth only after a long period of study. Epiphany described the process in which a person realized the truth in an instant.

In the history of Chinese Buddhist thought, Zhu Dao Sheng was the first thinker to discuss gradual study and epiphany. He said, "Epiphany means that one obtains the idea. Believing means that one believes what one hears. Believing is not real. Epiphany comes from the understanding of truth. Epiphany does not appear by itself. When epiphany comes out, believing will be replaced," (Hui Da, *Zhao Lun Shu*). In Dao Sheng's view, there were two kinds of knowledge. One was believing (*Xin*) or understanding by learning (*Wen Jie*), which was characterized with gradualness. It covered the knowledge one obtained through learning Buddhist classics. The other was epiphany (*Wu*) or realizing instantly (*Jian Jie*), which was characterized by enlightenment. It covered the deep understanding of truth in an instant. Dao Sheng stressed the latter.

Subsequently, Zen Buddhism inherited Zhu Dao Sheng's thoughts on this issue. Naturally, Zen Buddhism valued epiphany as it viewed that one's nature could be indicated by heart. Hui Neng clearly stated, "One's nature is Buddha. There will be no Buddha without

A Line-Carved Figure from the Qing Dynasty: Nanyue Huai Rang Monk, the 34th Patriarch. Huai Rang (677-744) was born in Jinkang, Jinzhou (today Shiquan County, Ankang, Sha'anxi Province). He was a student of Hui Neng Monk. His secular surname was Du. After Hui Neng died, Huai Rang succeeded him and taught Zen at Kwan-yin Terrace, Prajna Temple, Hengshan Mountain. Ma Zudao, his successor, fully developed a school of Zen called the Nanyue Sect. Huai Rang was revered as the founder of the Nanyue Sect.

207

human nature," (*Platform Sutra* [*Tan Jing*], *Bo Re Pin*). For Zen Buddhists, Buddha existed in one's heart. As a result knowledge was nothing but "Buddha in heart". Therefore, gradual study became insignificant and the epiphany of Buddha, which occurred in an instant, was what mattered. Hui Neng said, "If *prajna* (wisdom) appears, one's wrong ideas disappear instantly. One can realize Buddha if he understands his nature," (*Platform Sutra* [*Tan Jing*], *Bo Re Pin*). Shen Hui, a disciple of Hui Neng, explained this idea vividly: "Epiphany happens in a moment… it is like the threads of hemp that form a rope. When they are put on a wooden block, they can be cut by a sharp sword. Numerous as the threads are in number, they cannot stand the sword. It is equally true for one who hears Buddha," (*The Analects of Shen Hui*). Here, Shen Hui was comparing the moment when a person understands the truth to the instantaneous cutting of a hemp rope.

In the records of Huai Rang, a disciple of Hui Neng, gradual study was neglected while the importance of epiphany was stressed:

**Ma Zu lived in a temple on Hengshan Mountain. He meditated and neglected all who came to visit him, even his tutor… One day, his tutor was grinding a brick in front of the temple and Ma Zu did not see this. After a while, Ma Zu asked "What are you doing?" His tutor said, "Grinding it to make a mirror." Ma Zu said, "How can a brick be made into a mirror?" His tutor, "Since a brick cannot be made into a mirror, can you realize Buddha through meditation?" (*The Analects of Eminent Monks*, Vol. 1)**

Epiphany embodied something that we call intuition or inspiration today. It is the moment of inspiration that allows a person to get a fundamental understanding of something. As such, it involves the relationship between gradual study and fundamental progress. The concept was therefore of great importance to Chinese philosophers[42]. In other words, although ancient Chinese Zen Buddhism tended to neglect the gradual study of knowledge, its focus on epiphany has been an inspiration to many of the Chinese thinkers that have studied it.

---

42. It should be pointed out that in the history of Western philosophy, epiphany was noticed recently.

## Investigating Things and Gaining Knowledge

In the Song and Yuan dynasties, philosophers considered a third issue that related to the form or structure of knowledge, namely, investigating things and gaining knowledge. These ideas were first recorded in the Eight Terms (*Ba Tiao Mu*) in *Great Learning*: "One gains knowledge to investigate things and investigates things to gain knowledge." Philosophers focused on this issue during the Song and Ming dynasties.

In the commentary to *Great Learning*, Zhu Xi stated,

> **Investigating things and gaining knowledge means that one must approach the objects so as to gain knowledge of them. One's heart can understand things and things can embody some rules, which have not been fully recognized. Therefore, *Great Learning* aims firstly to teach learners how to approach things and discover truth based on the knowledge they have obtained. With long-time efforts, one can realize the truth embodied in things and solve all the problems. That's what I call gaining knowledge, the highest level of knowledge. (*Commentaries to Selected Great Learning*)**

Here, Zhu Xi was expressing three views. First, that knowledge is formed through one's contact with the objective world. Second, that the Buddhist view on epiphany should be embraced (he therefore also highlights the qualitative change that knowledge can bring). Third, knowledge dealt with the issues of the whole and the part, the phenomenon and the essence. Zhu Xi also described the relationship between the "method of getting knowledge" and the "result of knowledge" when he said, "One investigates one thing today and more tomorrow, then he will realize the truth someday," (*Questions in Great Learning*).

Wang Yangming disagreed with Zhu Xi's views and criticized him using the mentalist stance. He said: "In Zhu Xi's view, gaining knowledge means to discover the truth. However, to me, the truth about objects exists in one's heart, so to discover what one thinks is to discover the truth," (*The Analects of Wang Yangming* [*Chuan Xi Lu*], Vol. 2). Then, Wang Yangming stated his view: "To me, investigating things and gaining knowledge means that one's conscience is embodied by the

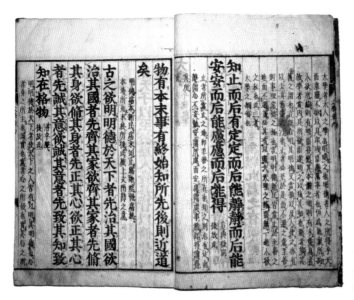

The discourse on "investigating things and gaining knowledge," in *Great Learning*, traditional thread binding.

object. One's conscience is the truth. When one's conscience is embodied in objects, the truth of all objects can be discovered. To discover one's conscience is gaining knowledge and to discover the truth in objects is investigating things," (*The Analects of Wang Yangming* [*Chuan Xi Lu*], Vol. 2). This makes it clear that, to Wang Yangming, investigating things and gaining knowledge meant to discover one's conscience, and to move from one's mind to external objects.

Wang Fuzhi deeply examined the relationship between investigating things and gaining knowledge:

> While investigating things, one uses the hearing, eyes, and ears, with learning in the first place and thinking in the second place. What one thinks is everything that one learns. While gaining knowledge, one uses the heart, with thinking in the first place and learning in the second place. What one suspects is everything that one learns. Gaining knowledge relies on investigating things. The heart controls the ears and the eyes. If the eyes and ears are dominant, the role of the heart will be abandoned. (*On Reading Four Classics, Great Learning*)

Wang Fuzhi's view was important. First, he combined investigating things and gaining knowledge with information and thinking, which enriched the ideas of perceptual knowledge and rational knowledge. Second, Wang Fuzhi discussed the relationship between investigating things and gaining knowledge in a dialectic and accurate way. This insight played an important role in the development of the ancient Chinese theory of knowledge.

## Removing Obstructions

Chinese philosophers realised that in order to obtain the right knowledge, one must use the right methods. One of the issues they discuss in relation to this challenge was removing obstructions. This issue was first mentioned by Chuang Tzu. In Pre-Qin times, it was reputed that there were one hundred Schools of Thought. The followers of these different schools disagreed over which school was right. As a result, Chuang Tzu said,

> The country suffers disturbance. The sages have not appeared and morality differs among the citizens. Some are complacent with their partial knowledge. Ears, eyes, noses, and mouths have their functions but cannot coordinate. Similarly, philosophers specialize in one field but cannot know all. (*Chuang Tzu, All under Heaven*)

To Chuang Tzu, the schools of thought expressed reasonable views but had only discovered partial truths. For Chuang Tzu they were guilty of dogmatism or *Qu* if they considered they had learnt all of the truth and that the other schools were wrong. What caused dogmatism? Chuang Tzu ascribed it to the partial understanding of knowledge. He explained this as follows:

> One cannot talk about the sea with a frog in well as it is limited by its environment. One cannot talk about ice with a summer insect as it is limited by its season. One cannot talk about Tao

**with a man in the countryside as he is limited by education. (*Qiu Shui*)**

Here, Chuang Tzu is using the frog in a well, the insect in summer, and the man in the countryside as representatives of one-sided thinking. Chuang Tzu's thoughts were valuable because dogmatism was prevalent in Chinese society through much of its history,

Later, Xun Zi expressed insightful views on removing obstructions. In *Removing Obstructions*, Xun Zi proposed the idea that: "Man's common fault is that he is limited by partial knowledge and unconscious of the complete truth." It is notable that Xun Zi inherited and extended Chuang Tzu's thoughts on this issue. Xun Zi said, "What will cause obstructions? Desire, hate, seeing the start only, seeing the end only, seeing the far only, seeing the near only, profound knowledge, superficial knowledge, knowing the past only, and knowing the present only." To sum up his views, he said, "There is difference among the objects in the world, which formed obstructions. This is the common fault in man's knowledge." Xun Zi also criticized one-sidedness and said that it caused obstruction: "Mo Zi values practice but neglects theory; Song Zi values desire but neglects the way; Shen Zi values situation but neglects knowledge; Hui Zi values language but neglects practice; Chuang Tzu values Tao but neglects human." These thought raise the question, "How could one avoid the one-sidedness?" Xun Zi said, "The sage realizes the harm of one-sidedness and obstruction in thinking, so he dislikes neither one thing nor another, overstates neither the start nor the end, stresses neither the near nor the far, overstates neither profundity nor superficiality, and stresses neither the past nor the present." Xun Zi's core idea was to "list both sides and make a criterion." In other words he stressed the all-sidedness of knowledge.

## Receptiveness and Serenity

To obtain "right knowledge", the ancient Chinese philosophers thought that a man must concentrate his attention, or practice what they called "receptiveness and serenity".

Lao Tzu was the first to notice the importance of receptiveness and serenity. He stressed that,

"One must remove distraction in the heart concealed by the secular world," (*Lao Tzu*, Chapter 10) so as to "achieve the receptiveness and serenity in mind," (Chapter 16). Chuang Tzu accepted Lao Tzu's thoughts and stressed the importance of the "serenity of mind" (*Xin Zhai*) and the "state of forgetting while sitting," (*Zuo Wang*). Chuang Tzu said,

Zhi Zhe Monk (538-597) was also known as Zhi Yi or Chen Dean (his secular name). He was founder of the Tiantai (Fahua) Sect of Chinese Buddhism.

> **Tao values receptiveness (*Xu*). Receptiveness means the serenity of the mind. (*Chuang Tzu, Conduct in Society*)**

> **Zuo Wang means one forgets his body and abandons his wisdom to break the bondage of the body and wisdom and achieve *Tao*. (*The Great and Most Honored Master*)**

Xun Zi examined the importance of receptiveness and serenity, with respect to gaining knowledge, in the most profound way. He proposed the idea or method of "observing objects with receptiveness, serenity and concentration," (*Xu Yi Er Jing*). He said,

> **How could people learn Tao? With the heart. How could the heart know Tao? With receptiveness, serenity and concentration. Receptiveness means one's ability to receive knowledge. Serenity means one's tranquil state of mind. Concentration means**

one's focus on one thing. (*Xun Zi, Removing Obstructions*)

The state of receptiveness, serenity and concentration marks great awakening. (*Removing Obstructions*)

In addition, the state of receptiveness, serenity, and concentration was considered to be the basic way to achieve *Tao*: "One who pursues but has not achieved *Tao* should depend on the state of receptiveness, serenity and concentration," (*Removing Obstructions*). In a word, it was thought that only through the state of receptiveness, serenity and concentration could man understand the world properly.

Receptiveness and serenity were an important thought in ancient Chinese Buddhism. Buddhists pursued a detachment from reality, which demanded that they realized truth in a state of purity. The basic way to achieve the required state was meditation. Meditation enabled people to calm themselves, to remove distractions and to possess wisdom. This resembled Chuang Tzu's *Zuo Wang* and *Xin Zhai*. Similarly, Hui Yuan, a monk from the Eastern Jin Dynasty proposed the "equal importance of Zen and wisdom" and Zhi Yi, a monk from the Sui Dynasty, proposed the concept of "meditation through serenity and observation." In the Song Dynasty, the Cheng-Zhu School viewed serenity as an important part of cultivation. In their theory of "cultivation via concentration" (*Zhu Jing Han Yang*), the key point of *Jing* was serenity. For instance, Zhu Xi said,

*Jing* (serenity) means that one restricts his desire and behavior so that he will not distract and indulge himself. (*Words of Zhu Zi*, Vol. 12)

*Jing* (serenity) is the state in which one always keeps conscious. (*Words of Zhu Zi*, Vol. 62)

It is therefore clear that the basic ways in which the different Chinese philosophies thought that people should obtain knowledge were consistent with each other.

# Views on Knowledge and Action

In ancient Chinese philosophy, views on knowledge and action concerned the relationship between knowledge and practice, especially the relationship between morality and practice. Obviously, these views were related to the Confucian ideal that one should possess the sage's virtue and practice the ruler's policy. It is of note that the relationship between knowledge and practice was a more prominent feature of ancient Chinese philosophy than it was of ancient Western philosophy.

## The Foundation of Early Views on Knowledge and Action

The knowledge-action issue was first mentioned in *Zuo Zhuan* and the *Book of Documents*. In *Zuo Zhuan*, it was said, "To obtain knowledge is not difficult. To act is," (*The 10th Year of the Reign of Duke of Zhao*). In the *Book of Documents* it was said, "What's difficult is not to obtain knowledge but to act," (*On the Effect of Fate*). Both sayings mean that it is more difficult to put knowledge into practice than it is to obtain knowledge.

In ancient China, knowledge and action were often thought of as being consistent and Ancient Chinese philosophers often mentioned them simultaneously. For instance, the Confucian view on knowledge and action was based on social morality. It was also common for ancient Chinese philosophers to participate in society while considering social issues. Confucius said, "When you are at home, be filial to your parents. When you are out, be respectful to your brothers." He also said, "When you have done this, you can learn knowledge," (*The Analects, Xue Er*). Here, being filial and respectful are both actions.

In Mohism, production was the most important issue related to the knowledge-action question.

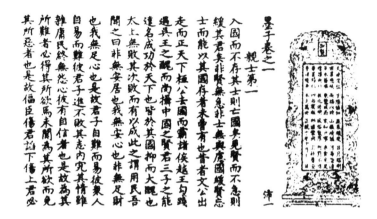

*Mo Zi* (Excerpt), printed in Ming Dynasty. *Mo Zi* was the representative work of Moism and compiled by students of Mo Zi. There were originally 71 articles. Now there are 53 existing articles.

Mo Zi said, "One who participates in production can survive and vice versa," (*Mo Zi, On Denying Music I*). In other words, Mohism viewed production as the most basic type of action. In spite of the fact that Confucianism and Mohism held different views on knowledge and action, they both valued knowledge and action (especially the latter). Confucianism highlighted "Knowledge, Action, Faith, and Honesty," (*Si Jiao*) (*The Analects, Xue Er*). Mohism, highlighted "Knowledge through hearing, seeing, and practicing," (*The Book of Mo Zi, Canon I*). Both Confucianism and Mohism united knowledge and action and noted the importance of action or practice. Confucian and Mohist views on knowledge and action were widely accepted by philosophers. Xun Zi viewed action as the highest level of knowledge: "To practice is better than to know; to know is better than to see; to see is better than to hear. The final stage of learning is to practice," (*Xun Zi, The Role of the Confucianist*). In addition, ancient Chinese philosophers noted two further things. First, that knowledge and action happened repeatedly. Confucius said, "Is it a pleasant thing one reviews what he has learnt?" (*The Analects, Xue Er*). Wang Chong said, "In Qi prefecture, people embroidered for generations and no woman could not. In Xiang prefecture, people brocaded for many years and the clumsy woman could. They saw and did day by day and became skillful," (*Critical Essays, Cheng Cai*). Second, that action could test knowledge. Han Fei said, "To test him with official post and performance," and "A prime minister starts from prefecture and a general starts from a soldier," (*Han Fei Zi, On Confucianism and Mohism*).

## Word and Action, Knowledge and Practice

It is notable that in ancient Chinese philosophy, two main questions were discussed in relation to knowledge and action, namely the relationships between words and actions and between knowledge and practice.

On the relationship between words and actions, philosophers widely believed that word must accord with action. For instance, Confucius said,

Now I hear what one says and see how one acts. (*The Analects, Gong Ye Chang*)

A gentleman views it as a shame when one brags but never acts. (*Xian Wen*)

Mo Zi said,

One must keep his words and act decidedly. The accordance between word and action is similar to that between tally (*Fu*) and symbol (*Jie*). (*Mo Zi, Universal Love II*)

A ruler must make his words consistent with his actions. (*Gong Meng*)

Xun Zi said, "One who acts in accordance with what he says is a treasure to a state; one who acts but does not say is a talent to a state; one who says but does not act is a citizen to a state; one who says good but does evil is a disaster to a state," (*Xun Zi, Strategies*). As can be seen, ancient Chinese philosophers thought that it was very important for there to be consistency between words and actions, and even viewed it as a moral issue. In fact, the consistency of words and actions was a traditional moral standard that was called Honesty (*Xin*). This idea was expressed in Confucianism in the phrase "Knowledge, Action, Faith, and Honesty". It was also expressed in Mo Zi's view that "One must keep his words and act decidedly." In addition, this moral standard accorded with epistemic law, or the unity of morality and wisdom.

CHINESE
PHILOSOPHY

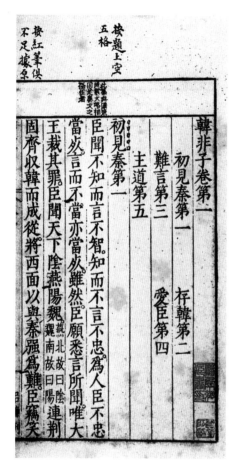

*Han Fei Zi* (Excerpt), printed in the reign of Emperor Wanli during the Ming Dynasty. *Han Fei Zi* was also called *Han Zi*. It was the representative work of Legalism in Pre-Qin times. It was the work of Han Fei, who inherited and developed the thoughts of Legalism.

At the same time, ancient Chinese philosophers observed that knowledge should be applied and not just obtained. Confucius said, "If a man who has read *Classic of Poetry* can neither handle state affairs nor answer questions fluently on diplomatic mission, what's the use of him reading so many books?" (*The Analects, Zi Lu*). Mo Zi said, "The words are unreal if one only says but does not act," (*Mo Zi, Geng Zhu*). In the late Warring States Period, Han Zi clarified this issue using a shooting metaphor:

**To judge words and action, one must take the real effect as one's criterion. One may hit the target with a new arrow. This does not mean that one is good at shooting as the target can be changed. When the target is five-*cun* in size and a man stands ten-foot away, he may hit the target even though he is not as skillful as Hou Yi and Feng Meng, as the target is unchanged. In this sense, when the target is unchanged, Hou Yi and Feng Meng can display their skill at five feet; when the target is changed, people will consider hitting the target a clumsy tactic. Now, people do not take the real effect as the criterion when they judge words and action. This is in vain though the words and action stand the test. (*Han Fei Zi, On the Debate Among the Schools of Thought*)**

Later, Wang Chong said, "A man is called sage

when he can put into practice what he has learnt. He is no different to a parrot that learns words if he just reads, even if he reads more than one thousand poems," (*Critical Essays, Supreme and Strange*). Obviously, ancient Chinese philosophers had fully realized that putting theory into practice was the real purpose of obtaining knowledge.

## Zhu Xi's View on Knowledge and Action

In the Song and Ming dynasties, views on knowledge and action developed in a more profound way. Zhu Xi was a representative philosopher of the Song Dynasty. His views can be summarized in two ways.

Zhu Xi (1130-1200), also known as Zhu Yuanhui and Zhu Hui'an, was born in Wuyuan, Huizhou (today in Jiangxi Province). He was a thinker, poet, philosopher, and a representative figure of the School of Mind during the Southern Song Dynasty.

First, he thought that knowledge and action depended on each other. While commenting on the *Doctrine of the Mean*, Zhu Xi related the following line to knowledge and action: "A gentleman should study extensively, inquire prudently, think carefully, distinguish clearly and practice earnestly." He said, "One studies, inquires, thinks and distinguishes, so he can choose the good things to learn. If one practices earnestly, he can always practice benevolence," (*Commentaries to Selected Doctrine of the Mean*). Here, Zhu Xi meant that the things a person studies, asks about, thinks about and distinguishes relate to knowledge, while the things a person practices relate to the appliance of knowledge. Zhu Xi thought that knowledge and action were interdependent. He noted, "Knowledge and action must rely on each other, like the eye and the foot. Without the foot, one cannot move; without the eye, one cannot see," (*Words of Zhu Zi*, Vol. 9). He also stressed

The *Commentaries to Selected Doctrine of the Mean, Commentaries to the Four Books*, printed in the Ming Dynasty, written by Zhu Xi in the Song Dynasty. The full title of the *Commentaries to the Four Books* was the *Commentaries to Selected Four Books*. It was a Confucian masterpiece that collected the *Four Books and Five Classics*. Zhu Xi first juxtaposed *Great Learning* and *Doctrine of the Mean* in *Book of Rites*, *The Analects* and *Mencius*. The annotations to *Great Learning* and *Doctrine of the Mean* were called *Zhang Ju* (Selected Annotations), while these to *The Analects* and *Mencius* were called *Ji Zhu* (Collected Annotation).

that: "Neither knowledge nor action should be overstated; otherwise both will be harmed," (*Words of Zhu Zi*, Vol. 9) and "When knowledge is clear, action will be well done, vice versa," (*Words of Zhu Zi*, Vol. 14). Evidently, Zhu Xi's view embodied the dialectic relationship between knowledge and action.

Second, Zhu Xi thought that knowledge appeared first and that action was more important. He said, "Knowledge appeared earlier than action while action was more important than knowledge," (*Words of Zhu Zi*, Vol. 9)? Zhu Xi explained this as follows:

**With knowledge, one can cultivate himself.**

**How could one act if he has not obtained knowledge?**

**To a walking man, how could he walk if he cannot see?** (*Words of Zhu Zi*, Vol. 9)

In contrast, Zhu Xi considered that: "One cannot act if he does not have knowledge and can act if he has," (*Works of Zhu Wen Gong*, Vo. 41). For Zhu Xi, it was action rather than knowledge that was most important. He said, "A sage firstly teaches knowledge, but he takes action as the final purpose," (*Works of Zhu Wen Gong*, Vo. 54). In addition, Zhu Xi observed that action tested whether one understood knowledge or not: "One has not obtained the knowledge if he cannot use it. This kind of knowledge is not real. There is no real knowledge that cannot be used," (*Works of Zhu*

*Wen Gong*, Vol. 72). It is noticeable that Zhu Xi mainly referred to moral knowledge or action. Zhu Xi's views were reasonable to some extent, however they were flawed as he confined himself to moral issues and failed to notice the importance of action in other fields.

## Wang Yangming's View on Knowledge and Action

Wang Yangming's view on knowledge and action countered that of Zhu Xi. It was representative of the views held during the Ming Dynasty. It can be summarized in two ways.

First, to counter Zhu Xi's view that knowledge and action were united, Wang Yangming proposed the unity of knowledge and action: "Knowledge and action are inseparable... Therefore, one makes progress by uniting them," (*The Analects of Wang Yangming* [*Chuan Xi Lu*], Vol. 2). How could knowledge and action be united? Wang Yangming answered this question as follows:

Wang Yangming (1472-1529), also known as Wang Shouren and Wang Bo'an, was born in Yuyao, Zhejiang Province. He was a philosopher and educator during the Ming Dynasty. He was the author of works such as *The Analects of Wang Yangming, Inquiry on the Great Learning* and *Collections of Mr. Yangming's Writings.*

**Knowledge guides action and action embodies knowledge. Knowledge is the start of action and action is the end of knowledge. (*The Analects of Wang Yangming* [*Chuan Xi Lu*], Vol. 1)**

**Action indicates to what extent one understands knowledge; knowledge indicates whether action is right. (*The Analects of Wang Yangming* [*Chuan Xi Lu*], Vol.2)**

Wang Yangming explained, "Knowledge and action tell the same meaning which consists of two sides," ("Reply to Friend"). As mentioned above, Wang Yangming's view was clear: Knowledge and action embodied and influenced each other. Action existed in knowledge and knowledge existed in action. In short, knowledge and action were indivisible.

Second, Wang Yangming thought that a person acted first before he learnt knowledge and that knowledge and action happened at the same time. Based on the view that knowledge and action were united, Wang Yangming stressed the importance of action. Unlike Zhu Xi, Wang Yangming observed that action appeared to precede knowledge. He used taste to explain this: "One knows the taste of food only after he has tasted it. How could he know that if he has not tasted it?" (*The Analects of Wang Yangming* [*Chuan Xi Lu*], Vol.2). He gave other examples such as: "One who learns to shoot must pull the bow and hit the target; one who learns calligraphy must prepare paper and ink and write in the wooden tablet with a brush; one who learns filiality must work hard and supports his parents." Therefore, he said that, "One could not obtain knowledge without action," (*The Analects of Wang Yangming* [*Chuan Xi Lu*], Vol.2). It was obvious that Wang Yangming's view embodied the idea that knowledge came from action. However, he was wrong to overstate the importance of action. By action, Wang Yangming meant morality (as did Zhu Xi). Therefore, to Wang Yangming, all human action was related to morality. He said, "When one sees a nice color, this is knowledge. When one likes this nice color, this is action. When one sees the nice color again and likes it, this is not because he sees the color," (*The Analects of Wang Yangming* [*Chuan Xi Lu*], Vol. 1). Wang Yangming clearly stated the importance and correctness of action. He further suggested, "One acts when there is an idea in his mind," (*The Analects of Wang Yangming* [*Chuan Xi Lu*], Vol. 3). This view fell into the trap of mentalism as it replaced action with subjective motivation (or will and spirit).

## Wang Fuzhi's View on Knowledge and Action

In the late Ming Dynasty and early Qing Dynasty, Wang Fuzhi expressed more profound views on knowledge and action. Wang Fuzhi inherited the reasonable views of his precursors and criticized them, forming his own mature views on knowledge and action. He stated that:

First, knowledge and action were different and supplementary. On the one hand, Wang Fuzhi disagreed with Zhu Xi's view that knowledge and action were separate. Wang Fuzhi believed that knowledge and action embodied each other. He said, "If one makes efforts, investigating things and gaining knowledge are both action. If one displays honesty, he can learn the knowledge in the world," (*Reading the Four Classics, Great Learning*). On the other, Wang Fuzhi also disagreed with Wang Yangming's view that knowledge and action were united. He stressed that knowledge and action belonged to different categories and that they had different functions. He said, "The difference between knowledge and action lies in the fact that knowledge pursues truth while action values the object," (*Reading the Four Classics, Doctrine of the Mean*). Evidently, Wang Fuzhi absorbed the reasonable elements and criticized the irrational elements in Zhu Xi and Wang Yangming's views (Zhu Xi stressed the difference between knowledge and action and neglected their unity, while Wang Yangming noticed their unity but neglected their differences). Wang Fuzhi further noted that: "One who knows that knowledge and action are supplementary as he knows that they are different," (*Commentaries to Selected Book of Rites, Doctrine of the Mean*). In other words, he thought that knowledge and action were both supplementary and different. Meanwhile, Wang Fuzhi observed that the relationship between knowledge and action changed and matured: "From knowledge one can know how to act and from action one can know what knowledge is. Then one can make progress," (*Reading the Four Classics, The Analects, Wei Zheng*). In this way, Wang Fuzhi discussed the dialectic relationship between knowledge and action.

Second, Wang Fuzhi stated that knowledge guided action and action tested knowledge. He elucidated the role and function of both knowledge and action: "For a gentleman, he acts based on knowledge," (*Note on Reading Classic of Poetry*, Vol. 1). In other words, knowledge could guide action and a man must have knowledge before he acted: "One must act after he has obtained knowledge and one acts in accordance with the knowledge he has," (*Notes on Four Classics*, Vol. 20). He also said:

Wang Fuzhi (1619-1692), also known as Wang Er'nong, Wang Jiangzhai, Yihu Taoist, and Mr. Chuanshan, was born in Hengyang, Hunan Province. He was a thinker and philosopher during the late Ming Dynasty and the early Qing Dynasty. He summarized the Schools of Mind of the Song and Ming dynasties while criticizing them and established the system of ancient Chinese philosophy. He was the author of the *External Commentaries on Book of Change*, the *Internal Commentaries on Book of Change*, the *Elaborations on the Book of Documents*, and many more.

"The more profound and accurate one's knowledge is, the more proper and reasonable one's action is." (*Reading the Four Classics, The Analects, Wei Zheng*) Nevertheless, Wang Fuzhi attached more importance to action. He considered action more important than knowledge and proposed the theory that action tested knowledge. He said, "Action can test knowledge while knowledge cannot test action," (*Elaborations on the Book of Documents, On the Effect of Fate II*) and "One who has knowledge may not act, but one who acts can know," (*Reading the Four Classics, The Analects, King Ling of Wei*). In detail, Wang Fuzhi discussed the role and function of action as follows: (1) One knew after he acted, or action was the source of knowledge. Wang Fuzhi said: "One learns Tao after he acts," (*Thoughts and Questions, Internal Chapters*). Here, Wang Fuzhi viewed action as the foundation of knowledge. (2) Knowledge ended with action, or action was the purpose of knowledge. Wang Fuzhi said, "The final end of knowledge is to practice it," (*Notes on Correcting the Unenlightened, Zhi Dang*). Here, Wang Fuzhi employed the idea of practice (*Elaborations on the Book of Documents, On the Effect of Fate II*) and the idea that "Action can indicate the power of knowledge," (*Notes on Four Classics*, Vol. 9). Wang Fuzhi put action on a higher level on which action embodied knowledge. In short, Wang Fuzhi's view on knowledge and action reached a profound level and embodied elements of both Chinese and Western philosophies.

# Appendix

## Chronological Table of the Chinese Dynasties

| | |
|---|---|
| Old Stone Age | Approx. 1,700,000-10,000 years ago |
| New Stone Age | Approx. 10,000-4,000 years ago |
| Xia Dynasty | 2070-1600 BC |
| Shang Dynasty | 1600-1046 BC |
| Western Zhou Dynasty | 1046-771 BC |
| Spring and Autumn Period | 770-476 BC |
| Warring States Period | 475-221 BC |
| Qin Dynasty | 221-206 BC |
| Western Han Dynasty | 206 BC-AD 25 |
| Eastern Han Dynasty | AD 25-220 |
| Three Kingdoms | AD 220-280 |
| Western Jin Dynasty | AD 265-317 |
| Eastern Jin Dynasty | AD 317-420 |
| Northern and Southern Dynasties | AD 420-589 |
| Sui Dynasty | AD 581-618 |
| Tang Dynasty | AD 618-907 |
| Five Dynasties | AD 907-960 |
| Northern Song Dynasty | AD 960-1127 |
| Southern Song Dynasty | AD 1127-1279 |
| Yuan Dynasty | AD 1206-1368 |
| Ming Dynasty | AD 1368-1644 |
| Qing Dynasty | AD 1616-1911 |
| Republic of China | AD 1912-1949 |
| People's Republic of China | Founded in 1949 |